The alien

The Lord will bring a
nation against your
Deut. 28:49

you to

the alien
the Lord
+ a
will bring a
nation

Sophia Press

the Mass
Bishop
Athanasius

2 Peter

History does not
repeat itself
but it Rymes

PRAISE FOR
GLORY UNTO GLORY

"Fr. Kirby's *Glory Unto Glory: A Primer on Ascetical Theology* is a classic for anyone aspiring to behold and affirm in their life 'the regenerative and transformative power of grace.' It is a rich resource serving classroom, retreat, and journal all in one. Fr. Kirby masterfully weaves together the Scriptures, the Catechism, elements of Christian Tradition, and personal stories to invite the reader to work more ardently at the supernatural life and to cooperate more fully with divine grace. There is so much here for the human heart."

—**MOST REVEREND DAVID BONNAR**, DD, bishop of Youngstown and editor of *The Priest Magazine*

"With *Glory Unto Glory*, Fr. Jeffrey Kirby provides all Christians, especially those called to marriage and family life, with an introduction to the supernatural life and the pursuit of holiness. This book is an important tool for our day, when the family has been so terribly under attack and we need an avenue to help us see once again the supernatural in the midst of the natural."

—**CARRIE GRESS**, author of *The Anti-Mary Exposed* and *Theology of Home*

"Fr. Kirby's book has the capacity to teach, challenge, and form the minds and hearts of a generation of Catholics who may simply not know where to begin. *Glory Unto Glory* has helped me to see the greater forest even amid the trees of daily life. When we know the 'whole story,' salvation becomes exciting and personal."

—**FR. JOHN PAUL MARY ZELLER**, Franciscan Missionaries of the Eternal Word

GLORY UNTO GLORY

Glory unto Glory

A Primer on
Ascetical Theology

FR. JEFFREY KIRBY

Angelico Press

First published in the USA
by Angelico Press 2022
Copyright © Fr. Jeffrey Kirby 2022

For information, address:
Angelico Press, Ltd.
169 Monitor St.
Brooklyn, NY 11222
www.angelicopress.com

paper 978-1-62138-823-4
Cloth 978-1-62138-824-1

Book and cover design
by Michael Schrauzer

To
Carole King,
Co-worker in Truth

TABLE OF CONTENTS

INTRODUCTION

IF YOU ARE LOOKING FOR THE riches of glory, the deep springs of our spiritual nature, and the full picture of the supernatural life given to us by God in Jesus Christ, then you have picked up the right book!

Many related books today limit themselves to the practice of prayer, or a broad introduction to the spiritual life, or some address moral truth, but few—if any—contemporary books place all these different aspects within the gift of our supernatural lives. If we don't have a full grasp of our ultimate call, namely, to live a supernatural life, to share in God's own divine nature by the merits of Jesus Christ and the workings of his grace, then our efforts in the spiritual life, or our struggles with prayer or virtue, would lack a definitive direction and purpose. We wouldn't truly understand what we were laboring for and seeking to receive by grace. Our vision would be severely hindered and we wouldn't fully know what we were doing or why it was significant.

This book offers the big picture, the infinite horizon, of the supernatural life. It provides the oftentimes missing context within which all the other various parts of what it means to be made in the image and likeness of God are contained and receive their full meaning and purpose. For this reason, the book has been entitled *From Glory Unto Glory*. The title comes from a description of the supernatural life by the Apostle Saint Paul:

And all of us, with unveiled faces, seeing the glory of the Lord as though reflected in a mirror, are being transformed into the same image from one degree of glory to another; for this comes from the Lord, the Spirit. (2 Cor 3:18)

This study of the supernatural life, and the dissection of the different truths relating to it, is formally called ascetical theology. The word "ascetical" means the denial of oneself, the acceptance of spiritual death to our "old self" so that a "new self" can be brought forth, for the purpose of being made like God in Jesus Christ and so share in the divine glory forever.

Ascetical theology is vastly different from the various forms of "spiritual theology" that are found in theological circles and publishing houses today. Most of those fields are predominantly focused on prayer and its methods. They tend to have a very subjective component and are inclined to neglect dogmatic and moral theology. Ascetical theology, on the contrary, is the well-spring from which the doctrinal teachings of the Church consistently and beautifully flow. It is theologically holistic and objective in its approach.

Ascetical theology is the heart that sustains and unites right belief (doctrine) and right action (moral truth). It is the theological science behind the expression, "The early Fathers learned their theology on their knees." Its preeminence is expressed by the Latin maxim: *Lex orandi, lex credendi, lex vivendi,* namely, the law of prayer is the law of belief is the law of living.

And so, let's begin our study of the supernatural life. The human person is made by and for God.

This simple truth is debated by some and ignored by many in the West today. Its power and importance, however, goes beyond the momentary disputes and disbelief of any age.

Acknowledged or not, we were made by God and we were made for him. We share in God's own divine life. We do not merit and are not entitled to it. The supernatural life, which is a sharing in the divine nature, is a free gift that is given to every human being. It was lost but has been restored to us in Jesus Christ.

Each of us comes from the mind of God and each of us will one day stand before him in judgment. We will either share in his glory or be eternally dismissed from his presence. The task of our lives, therefore, is to understand our beginning and our end.

We are called to use the awareness of our origin and finality to propel us to Jesus Christ. It is our summons to accept and reciprocate God's love in this life, share communion with him in Jesus Christ, live by his moral law, cooperate with his grace, and so allow our supernatural lives to flourish and be made fit to share in God's everlasting glory. It is precisely the nurturing of the supernatural life here in time and space that will permit us, by God's goodness, to enter into a full sharing of that life in heaven.

THE EXAMPLE OF SAINT PAUL

The process described above can be found in the life of Saint Paul. The persecutor of the early Church was awakened by the Lord Jesus and invited to follow him (see Acts 9:1–22). He describes the unmerited kindness of the Lord and the call to follow him.

The saying is sure and worthy of full acceptance, that Christ Jesus came into the world to save sinners—of whom I am the foremost. But for that very reason I received mercy, so that in me, as the foremost, Jesus Christ might display the utmost patience, making me an example to those who would come to believe in him for eternal life. (1 Tim 1:15-16)

After the acceptance of God's love and the invitation of the Lord Jesus to follow him, there is a denial of oneself and a surrender of our lives to the way of the Lord Jesus. Saint Paul explains,

I have been crucified with Christ; and it is no longer I who live, but it is Christ who lives in me. And the life I now live in the flesh I live by faith in the Son of God, who loved me and gave himself for me. (Gal 2:19b-20)

After the spiritual death to ourselves, the grace of God is able to transform us, and God is able to reveal himself to us in Jesus Christ. Saint Paul describes this powerful unveiling.

And all of us, with unveiled faces, seeing the glory of the Lord as though reflected in a mirror, are being transformed into the same image from one degree of glory to another; for this comes from the Lord, the Spirit. (2 Cor 3:18)

This is the path and the process of the grace of God in Jesus Christ. It is a slow journey that's marked by a molding and transforming of our personhood in a way that makes us fit to share in the eternal glory of God.

We need to understand the truths and the phases of this journey.

STEP BY STEP

As a help in understanding our supernatural life and its transformation, the different chapters of this book will systematically walk us through the different truths of ascetical theology. The chapters will cover: our First Inheritance, our Rebellion and the Fall from Grace, our Redemption in Jesus Christ, Divine Grace, and the Purgative Way.

Each of the chapters will progressively explore and teach us the different aspects of the supernatural life. The chapters and their teachings intersect and show us the inner harmony of the redeeming process by which our supernatural lives are converted, healed, transformed by grace, and made to share in God's glory forever in Jesus Christ.

STRUCTURE OF THE CHAPTERS

As you walk through the book, each chapter follows a similar structure. Each chapter will have a pastoral story or situation, a thorough teaching on a particular part of the supernatural life presented within a biblical context, and then a very important application section entitled *Taking It to Heart.*

The application section consists of suggestions for prayer, an examination of conscience, and other spiritual resources from the Church's treasury. The section is meant to guide you into living out the teaching that's given in the respective chapter.

It is very important that the lessons of this book are not kept as intellectual fodder, or as spiritual meanderings, or as a loosely provided inspiration for the mere satisfaction of our emotions. The teachings presented in this book pertain to our spiritual souls and the well-spring of the supernatural life within us. The chapters, and the truths they present, are meant to be taken seriously. They must be reflected upon and actively applied to our lives today as we seek to live the supernatural life in Jesus Christ.

LET'S START AT THE BEGINNING

With this introduction completed, let's move to the beginning. Not just to our first chapter, but to the very beginning of creation. We begin with our first inheritance.

CHAPTER ONE

Our First Inheritance

They heard the sound of the LORD God walking in the garden at the time of the evening breeze, and the man and his wife hid themselves from the presence of the LORD God among the trees of the garden.

Genesis 3:8

THE STORY BEHIND THE CANOPY

WALKING DOWN THE GRAND center aisle of Saint Peter's Basilica in Rome, a pilgrim comes across the main altar, the Altar of the Confession, with its magnificent canopy. The altar is the heart of the basilica, as the sacred actions celebrated upon it are the summit and source of the Mystical Body of Christ.

Built directly over the very bones of Saint Peter, the chief apostle of the Lord Jesus, the altar is named after the apostle's declaration of faith: "You are the Messiah, the Son of the living God" (Mt 16:16).

In approaching so splendid a place, we can understandably miss a blatant symbol of the ascetical life on the columns of the canopy of this holy altar. Moving closer to the columns, we see a crest composed of the three familiar bees representing the Barberini family, who commissioned the canopy. If we look closely, above the family crest, we see a woman's face. As we circle the altar clockwise, and note the image of the woman's face on each of the columns, she moves from peace, to joy, to distress. Pain seems to abate and intensify. What is happening to this woman?

The woman is in the pleasure and pain of childbirth. The natural process comes to fruition at the end of the cycle where, instead of a woman's face, we see the beaming, smiling face of her newborn baby.

Why is such a scene on the very base of the columns of the main altar of this great basilica?

God desires to be in union with us. He uses the natural order to give grace and express supernatural truths. As two became one, and the woman brought forth new life, so we are called to seek to be one with God and allow for a new creation to come forth within us (cf. Rom 8:23; Eph 4:20–24; Gal 2:20).

This was the original union given to our first parents. It's the supernatural life. It's the union that is a part of our first inheritance. Since we were born after the Fall from grace, it's easy to be unaware of our original holiness, since we only know our fallen nature and the struggle for holiness and union with God.

In the beginning, however, it was not so. The turmoil and the battle are not the way God wanted us to live. It's essential, therefore, that we understand the original justice of our human nature, so that we can praise God for his original plan, realize what sin has taken from us, and learn what we can regain by the grace of God in Jesus Christ.

As a help for us to understand the supernatural life, this chapter will explore the first inheritance offered to the human family. It will dive into areas of our human nature that we couldn't imagine or that we never thought possible.

> See, this alone I found, that God made human beings straightforward, but they have devised many schemes. (Eccles 7:29)

OUR ORIGINAL INHERITANCE

While in the seminary at the North American College in Rome, I was able to meet many prestigious theologians, philosophers, historians, and artists. As the center of the Church, Rome draws everyone who has something to say or contribute to our tradition in some form or fashion. Many times, these luminaries host a talk, presentation, or display. In these ways, even lowly seminarians could meet great men and women.

On one such occasion, a noted theologian was giving a talk at one of the universities and was staying at our seminary. During one of the meals, I was able to sit at his table. It was a high honor, or so I thought, and I was eager to hear his wisdom and insights.

As the conversation moved along, the topic of fallen human nature came up. The theologian abruptly stopped the discussion and told us, "Such language isn't helpful. The classification of 'fallen' implies a previous state of nature and such arguments are no longer helpful to theological debate."

Many of us were silent after his comments. Didn't the Church teach an original justice of our human nature before the Fall? Isn't that precisely what our nature "fell" from?

Eventually, a brave seminarian among us spoke up. "I must be misunderstanding your point. Are you saying the language is no longer helpful on its own, or are you saying there was no original holiness of our human nature?"

The theologian looked sickened by the question. There was an awkward pause and then he told us, "I do not adhere to the notion of a previous state of human nature. Our nature is what it is. Our best efforts are to reflect upon that reality and show how theology can help us find the presence of God and the meaning of our lives."

The rather eloquent answer was followed by silence. There were no follow-up questions or comments and the meal concluded shortly afterward. Later, as the other seminarians at the table and I spoke about it, we expressed the shock it was to us that a high-profile theologian of the Church would deny a basic, initial truth of the Church and of her theology.

As I have studied theology since and have made my rounds to theological meetings and conferences, it has become painfully obvious that many theologians, especially in the fields of ascetical ("spiritual") and moral theology, do not believe, acknowledge, or base their teachings on an original holiness of human nature.

The consequences are dire.

If we fail to comprehend the original holiness and justice of our human nature, then we cannot grasp the original plan of God for the human family. In addition, we will falsely believe that fallen humanity is the sum definition of our nature, as if sin is the source of our identity as human beings. Lastly, if we do not know our first inheritance, we cannot fully realize the privation and wickedness of sin.

If we witness evil in our world and say out loud, "We're only human. That's human nature," we erroneously make sin a type of synonym for our human nature. No, sin is not who we are as human beings. We can see the evil and sin of our world and rightly observe, "Such is *fallen* human nature," since we are made good and reflect this true identity when we seek holiness, exercise virtue, and do good deeds. When we sin, it's a reflection of our fallenness, not of our human nature.

By recognizing our original holiness, we can come to a more profound awareness of the infinite goodness and sublime benevolence of the living God. We are filled with genuine awe at our own creation. We see our dignity as human beings in a stunningly new way, as we grieve the loss we have suffered as a race. We come to a broader and more penetrating realization of the horrors of original sin and what sin has taken from us. In knowing our original holiness and justice, we understand what was taken. We grieve the loss of the world that God desired for us. We mourn the forfeiture of our original innocence to sin. And, in the original sin, we see the tragic source of every actual sin throughout human history and we realize the terrible consequences of sin upon our nature.

For these reasons, and many others, we need to know the original holiness of our human nature. What was it? What did it involve? What did it look like?

> The Church, interpreting the symbolism of biblical language in an authentic way, in the light of the New Testament and Tradition, teaches that our first parents, Adam and Eve, were constituted in an original "state of holiness and justice." This grace of original holiness was "to share in . . . divine life." (*Catechism of the Catholic Church* 375, hereafter *CCC*)

ORIGINAL HOLINESS AND JUSTICE

In this context, when we speak of "holiness," we are referring to God's own life within us. When we speak of "justice" in this context, we are referring to a holistic integrity of our human nature as a gift from God's divine love.

The original holiness and justice of our human nature was comprised of many gifts from God. These included: (A) the supernatural gift of sanctifying grace and its holiness; and, (B) the preternatural gifts and original justice.

Such supernatural and preternatural gifts can be discerned and recognized within the figurative language of the Book of Genesis. While the portion of Genesis that relates to our original inheritance uses symbolic language, it still very much communicates divine truth relating to our original holiness and justice. Such truth can be identified within the written Word of God and then interpreted and developed within the perennial wisdom of Sacred Tradition and the constant theological tradition of the Church.

As we approach the gifts of our original inheritance and seek to explore their meaning, we need to define and distinguish between "supernatural" and "preternatural."

▶ Supernatural: A gift that is infinitely above our nature. "Super" is Latin for "above."

▶ Preternatural: A gift that goes beyond what is due to our nature but does not surpass the capabilities of a created nature. "Preter" is Latin (*praeter*) for "beyond."

With these definitions clarified, we can now dive into the original holiness and justice of our nature and seek to understand each of these respective gifts from God.

> The first man was not only created good, but was also established in friendship with his Creator and in harmony with himself and with the creation around him, in a state that would be surpassed only by the glory of the new creation in Christ. (CCC 374)

THE SUPERNATURAL GIFT OF SANCTIFYING GRACE

In the beginning of time, God created the heavens and the earth. He crowned his creation with the human person, made in his image and likeness, destined to share his divine nature as a true son by sanctifying grace.

The Book of Genesis describes the perfect architectural plan of God in creating the world (Chapter 1). Each successive "day" is a figurative expression of the orderly, hierarchical development of creation that led to a world ready for humanity. The human body developed within the context of the material world (cf. 1:26; 2:7). When God's providence determined it, the body was wedded with a spiritual soul (2:7–8). Not solely of the earth, the human person held the "breath of life" and was placed—body and soul—within a world that was molded and fashioned for him (2:7–8, 15). He was both matter and spirit. He was body, but also a spiritual soul.

Consisting of a body and soul, the human person was fearfully and wonderfully made (see Ps 139). Although a majestic microcosm of spirit and matter, human nature—of itself—would still only have been of the natural order.

In his loving kindness, however, God endowed our human nature with sanctifying grace. While such grace does not make us God, it does dramatically transform us and make us God-like. With sanctifying grace, we are able to share in God's own divine nature. As a sheer act of goodness on the part of God, we are elevated to a supernatural relationship with him. We become justified, a partaker of the divine nature, an adopted son of God, and an heir to eternal life.

Of itself in the natural state, our nature could not have achieved such blessedness. Such a sanctification could only have come from God, and he generously gave it as a gratuitous gift.

The Book of Genesis figuratively describes the gift of sanctifying grace by recording that our first parents were made in God's own image and likeness: "So God created humankind in his image, in the image of God he created them; male and female he created them" (1:27). No other creature was described in this way. It was unique and beyond the scope of creation, even of human nature itself. This was an endowment beyond expectation.

The fullest meaning of this biblical description can be found later in Genesis, when we're told that Adam "became the father of a son in his likeness, according to his image, and named him Seth" (5:3).

The expressions "image" and "likeness," therefore, express sonship. Made in God's image and likeness, our first parents were the son and daughter of God by grace. They were blessed to be in communion with God as their loving Father. We see here the biblical testimony of sanctifying grace.

In addition, we are given a passing glimpse of the intimacy between God and our first parents. The Book of Genesis tells us that Adam and Eve heard "the LORD God walking in the garden at the time of the evening breeze" (3:8). God was coming to be with them, to take an evening stroll with them. The small reference is a figurative reflection of the close relationship our first parents had with God through sanctifying grace.

Of all the other gifts given by God in our original inheritance, none of them could ever compare with sanctifying grace. It is God calling us to himself and making us capable of accepting the summons and being in a relationship with him.

If we do not understand sanctifying grace, then we cannot understand the meaning, purpose, and value of the supernatural life, the ascetical life, or the life of prayer. Everything begins (or ends) with sanctifying grace.

THE ORIGINAL INTEGRITY OF THE PRETERNATURAL GIFTS

As God created our human nature and endowed us with sanctifying grace, so he also blessed us with the original integrity of the preternatural gifts. It was only the presence of sanctifying grace that made our human nature capable of receiving the three preternatural gifts. They were given by God and endowed us with an "integrity," an internal union, wholeness, and integration within ourselves.

The preternatural gifts were not supernatural, since they were not infinitely above our human nature. They were certainly beyond the actual needs of our nature, but they did not surpass the capabilities of created nature. For example, the angels have these gifts as a part of their angelic nature, which is beyond human nature, but is still a created nature nonetheless (and not a divine nature). Simply put, the preternatural gifts were beyond our human nature, but God originally gave them to humanity to help us fully love him and be in a relationship with him.

The three preternatural gifts were:

Infused Knowledge. Left to our own abilities, we receive knowledge only slowly and oftentimes with great effort. God, therefore, blessed our human nature with an infusion of the knowledge of the things that are indispensable for us to live according to the laws of reason. Infused knowledge gave humanity religious and moral knowledge, as well as any material and technical knowledge that was necessary to fulfill the needs of our human estate. This gift is oftentimes called "the privilege of the angels," since the angels possess it as a normative part of their nature.

Integrity of the Passions. Left to our own abilities, there is a struggle between the passions of our lower soul and the reason of our higher soul. God, therefore, blessed our human nature with a harmony between our passions and our reason. Reason ordered our passions, and our passions obeyed and assisted with the powers of our reason. Our intellect and will were directed by truth and not easily swayed by a craving for pleasure. There was no inclination to evil and no indulgence to its lies and empty promises. Decisions were made within the power of reason, rather than the wayward desires of our passions. Such a gift did not make it impossible for humanity to sin, but it made the exercise of virtue easier and the allure of sin less enticing. Ascetical theology calls this gift "perfect rectitude." For example, some of these gifts are held by the angels as a part of their angelic nature.

Immortality of the Body. Left to our own abilities, we are subject to sickness and death. God, therefore, blessed our human nature with a co-sharing of our body in the immortality of our higher, spiritual soul. Our bodies were raised to the level of our souls and they would not suffer disease, illness, or physical death. God did not want his children to endure bodily suffering, death, and the death of their loved ones. Imagine a world without heart disease, Alzheimer's, and cancer. Imagine a world without death or the grieving of loved ones. This is the world God wanted for us. It's the one he gave us in the beginning. The angels do not have material bodies but possess immortality as a part of their normative nature.

Revelation makes known to us the state of original holiness and justice of man and woman before sin: from their friendship with God flowed the happiness of their existence in paradise. (*CCC* 384)

The figurative language of the Book of Genesis describes these gifts in this way.

Infused knowledge. In terms of religious truth, the sacred narrative explains the infused knowledge of our first parents. Throughout Genesis, Chapters 1–3, God spoke to Adam and Eve and they understood him. They knew who God was, that he loved them, and that they were to love him in return and obey him. They did not view him as a stranger, but truly knew him. He was not approached with suspicion or confusion. In Genesis, Chapter 2, where the creation of humanity is described in greater detail, God is even called by his personal, familial name "Yahweh," rather than the generic name "Elohim" (which just means "God"). The name indicates the knowledge our first parents had of God and their clear awareness of their status as his children by grace. Furthermore, when Adam and Eve named their son Seth, they indicated an awareness of the sonship to God. By the sacred narrative using the same terms "image" and "likeness" for Seth as had been used for Adam and Eve, a clear connection is made between Seth's sonship to Adam and Eve and our first parent's own sonship to God (see 5:3).

In addition, God gave Adam and Eve commands and they understood them. In terms of moral knowledge, when God gave the instruction against eating from the Tree of the Knowledge of Good and Evil, our first parents understood the command (see 2:16–17). In terms of material and technical knowledge, at the beginning of time, when the care of the land was completely new, God placed Adam and Eve in the garden and told them to care for the earth and they knew how to do it (see 2:15). Adam also held the knowledge of every living thing and was able to utter their names (see 2:19–20).

In these ways, we see how the figurative language of the Book of Genesis helps us to understand the preternatural gift of infused knowledge.

The Lord created human beings out of earth,
    and makes them return to it again.
He gave them a fixed number of days,
    but granted them authority over everything on
        the earth.
He endowed them with strength like his own,
    and made them in his own image.
He put the fear of them in all living beings,
    and gave them dominion over beasts and birds.
Discretion and tongue and eyes,
    ears and a mind for thinking he gave them.
He filled them with knowledge and understanding,
    and showed them good and evil.
He put the fear of him into their hearts
    to show them the majesty of his works.
And they will praise his holy name,
    to proclaim the grandeur of his works.
He bestowed knowledge upon them,
    and allotted to them the law of life.
He established with them an eternal covenant,
    and revealed to them his decrees.
Their eyes saw his glorious majesty,
    and their ears heard the glory of his voice.
He said to them, "Beware of all evil."
    And he gave commandment to each of them
        concerning the neighbor.
Their ways are always known to him;
    they will not be hid from his eyes.

He appointed a ruler for every nation,
    but Israel is the Lord's own portion.
All their works are as clear as the sun before him,
    and his eyes are ever upon their ways.
Their iniquities are not hidden from him,
    and all their sins are before the Lord.
One's almsgiving is like a signet ring with the Lord,
    and he will keep a person's kindness like the
        apple of his eye.
Afterward he will rise up and repay them,
    and he will bring their recompense on their
        heads.
Yet to those who repent he grants a return,
    and he encourages those who are losing hope.

                      Sirach 17:1–24

Integrity of the Passions. The harmony between the
passions and our reason is seen in the response of
Adam when he saw Eve: "This at last is bone of my
bones and flesh of my flesh" (2:23). He immediately
saw her as his equal. In the figurative language of
the sacred narrative, she was not taken from his foot
or from his head. She is not his inferior or superior.
She was taken from his side (2:21–22). She is his
equal. In seeing Eve naked, and knowing of his own
nakedness, he saw the immediate complementarity
of body and could discern the complementarity of
soul. There was no shame in their mutual nakedness.
Adam's reaction was not one of lust or uncontrolled
desire. The attraction was born of reason and a
desire for companionship of body and soul.

    In this most intimate of relationships, we
clearly see a reflection of the overall integrity of

the passions that existed within our first parents. There was a peace between desire and decision, the passions and our reason.

> Wisdom protected the first-formed father of the
>   world,
> when he alone had been created;
> she delivered him from his transgression,
> and gave him strength to rule all things.
>   Wisdom 10:1-2

Immortality of the Body. In the figurative language of the Book of Genesis, we are told of God's gift of immortality to the human body. The gift is indirectly recounted as God tells Adam and Eve: "And the LORD God commanded the man, 'You may freely eat of every tree of the garden; but of the tree of the knowledge of good and evil you shall not eat, for in the day that you eat of it you shall die'" (2:16-17). The warning of the possibility of death indicates a pre-existing immortality. God is warning our first parents of the possibility of not only spiritual death, but of a physical death (see 3:19).

In our original inheritance, God did not want us to experience disease, hardship, and death (see 3:16-19 for the sufferings after the Fall). He wanted our bodies to share in the immortality of our spiritual souls.

The Book of Wisdom helps us to understand the Genesis account. It teaches us: "Thus they reasoned, but they were led astray, for their wickedness blinded them, and they did not know the secret purposes of God, nor hoped for the wages of holiness, nor discerned the prize for blameless souls; for God created us for incorruption, and made us in the image of his own eternity, but through the devil's envy death entered the world, and those who belong to his company experience it" (2:21–24).

> "You are from your father the devil, and you choose to do your father's desires. He was a murderer from the beginning and does not stand in the truth, because there is no truth in him. When he lies, he speaks according to his own nature, for he is a liar and the father of lies." (Jn 8:44)

These were the three preternatural gifts of our original integrity. God blessed us with infused knowledge, an integrity of the passions, and an immortality of the body. Such gifts were meant as "extra helps" beyond our nature to build us up so that we could respond and cooperate with sanctifying grace and so love God and live in a loving union with him as our Father.

It must be stressed, however, that while the preternatural gifts were amazing and inspiring of themselves, they were infinitely subordinate to sanctifying grace. The preternatural gifts were in service to our supernatural life, which we received solely by sanctifying grace.

> By the radiance of this grace all dimensions of man's life were confirmed. As long as he remained in the divine intimacy, man would not have to suffer or die. The inner harmony of the human person, the harmony between man and woman, and finally the harmony between the first couple and all creation, comprised the state called "original justice."

> The "mastery" over the world that God offered man from the beginning was realized above all within man himself: *mastery of self.* The first man was unimpaired and ordered in his whole being because he was free from the triple concupiscence that subjugates him to the pleasures of the senses, covetousness for earthly goods, and self-assertion, contrary to the dictates of reason. (CCC 376–377)*

APPLICATION: TAKING IT TO HEART

Having explored the original holiness and justice of our human nature, we can now apply these truths to the ascetical life and see how they can help us to grow in our supernatural life with God.

The following spiritual exercises are suggested as helps in the work of the ascetical life.

Focus from the Holy Mass

Reflect upon the *Domine, non sum dignus* prayer of the Mass: "Lord, I am not worthy that you should enter under my roof, but only say the word and my soul shall be healed."

Consider: 1) We are not worthy of a relationship with God; 2) God blessed us with holiness and justice at the beginning of time so that we could be with him; 3) We rebelled against our Father and his gifts, but he sent his Son to redeem us, heal us, and reconcile us to himself.

---

* Unless otherwise indicated, italics appearing in citations also appear in the original texts.

Lectio Divina *Suggestion*

Spend some time, perhaps five to fifteen minutes, repeating and breathing into your heart the following portion of the living Word of God: "They said to him, 'Why then did Moses command us to give a certificate of dismissal and to divorce her?' He said to them, 'It was because you were so hard-hearted that Moses allowed you to divorce your wives, but from the beginning it was not so. And I say to you, whoever divorces his wife, except for unchastity, and marries another commits adultery'" (Mt 19:7–9).

Consider: While the Lord Jesus is giving a teaching on divorce, he references the beginning of creation. Reflect upon those powerful words: "but from the beginning it was not so." As the Lord Jesus goes back to the beginning of creation to show that divorce was not a part of God's original plan, consider how the loss of our original holiness and justice were not a part of God's original plan. Reflect upon the world that God wanted for us and gave to us before we introduced the corrosion of sin.

Meditation Theme

Use your spiritual imagination and compose a place. Imagine the sights, smells, sounds, taste, and touch of the environment. Allow yourself to be truly, spiritually present in that moment.

Compose the Garden of Eden. Imagine the bushes, layers of grass, the bright colors of the foliage, and fruit hanging from trees everywhere. Smell the freshness of the garden, the roses and budding flowers. Hear the sounds of beloved animals and the buzzing of bees. Feel the grass on your toes, feel the bark of the trees, and taste the ripe fruit in your hand and mouth. As you compose the place, imagine the preternatural gifts in your soul. Then, when you're ready, feel the power of sanctifying grace. Imagine God coming to you in the breeze of the evening. Hear the breeze, feel it on your body, let God come and walk with you. Identify the abundance of blessings throughout your body and soul as the living God walks with you and loves you. When the time is right, begin your colloquy, your conversation with him. Ask him the questions on your heart. Listen quietly. Love deeply. Know that God is with you.

Poustinia Meditation

This method is different from other forms of prayer. The task is to clear your mind of all thoughts and attempt to think of nothing other than a simple word. It can be repeated multiple times or simply held in our minds. Sometimes the use of a foreign word can help us stay focused. For our exercise today, focus on the word: "Iustitia" (Latin for "justice"), or another word that stood out to you during this chapter.

Examination of Conscience

Do I realize how much God truly loves me and wants a familial relationship with me?

Do I grasp the infinite value of sanctifying grace?

Have I grieved the loss of our original holiness?

Do I let myself reflect on what we lost in the preternatural gifts?

Do I remind myself of God's original plan when the fallenness of the world causes me sorrow?

Do I seek to realize fully what Jesus Christ has done
for me by his redemption of humanity?

Do I labor against the fallenness of my passions?

Do I seek discipline from God when I have sinned
against him or a neighbor?

Do I cling to the sacraments of the New Covenant, as
the source of sanctifying grace today?

Do I pine for the eternal happiness of Heaven?

Suggested Saints and Holy Ones

The Tradition of the Church has always held that our
first parents, Adam and Eve, were ransomed by the
Lord Jesus and brought into heaven during the "Har-
rowing of Hell" on the original Holy Saturday. As such,
we can turn to our first earthly father and our first
earthly mother and pray to them, seek their spiritual
friendship, and ask for their intercession. They know
the anguish of rejecting God's fellowship, the goodness
of his discipline, and the joys of his presence forever.

We can also pray to righteous Abel, who was raised
by our first parents and was the tragic first victim of
violence in human history. We can turn to him and
ask for his supplication and guidance as we seek to
live lives of peace and harmony with God and our
neighbor.

> The patriarchs, prophets, and certain other Old
> Testament figures have been and always will be
> honored as saints in all the Church's liturgical tra-
> ditions. (CCC 61)

Three Prayers from Our Tradition

ACT OF FAITH

O my God, I firmly believe
  that you are one God in three divine Persons,
  Father, Son, and Holy Spirit.
I believe that your divine Son became man
  and died for our sins and that he will come
  to judge the living and the dead.
I believe these and all the truths
  which the Holy Catholic Church teaches
  because you have revealed them
  who are eternal truth and wisdom,
  who can neither deceive nor be deceived.
In this faith I intend to live and die.
Amen.

SAINT MICHAEL
THE ARCHANGEL PRAYER

Saint Michael the Archangel,
  defend us in battle.
Be our protection against the wickedness
  and snares of the devil;
May God rebuke him, we humbly pray;
And do thou, O Prince of
  the Heavenly Host,
by the power of God,
thrust into hell Satan and all evil spirits,
who wander through the world
  for the ruin of souls.
Amen.

PRAYER TO SAINT JOSEPH
FOR A HAPPY DEATH

O Blessed Joseph,
you gave your last breath in the loving
    embrace of Jesus and Mary.
When the seal of death shall close my life,
come with Jesus and Mary to aid me.
Obtain for me this solace for that hour—
to die with their holy arms around me.
Jesus, Mary, and Joseph,
I commend my soul, living and dying, into
    your sacred arms.
Amen.

CHAPTER TWO

Our Rebellion and the Fall from Grace

But the LORD God called to the man, and said
to him, "Where are you?" He said, "I heard the
sound of you in the garden, and I was afraid,
because I was naked; and I hid myself."

Genesis 3:9–10

A BEAUTIFUL TEMPLE

IMAGINE AN ARCHITECT WHO FASH-
ioned a beautiful, harmonious temple. Imagine the
majesty of the compact stone, the marble, the pil-
lars, the symmetrical interior, the splendor and nobility
of the entire structure. Its perfection is a cry for the
praise and glory of God. Everything about the temple
speaks of elegance and refinement. It's a perfection of
artisanship. It's stately and awesome to behold. It's a
testament of creativity and love.

Now imagine if someone were to live in this exalted
temple. Imagine if someone were to hand him a grenade, which he held in the middle of the magnificent
temple. Imagine the grenade exploding and the severity

of the blast ripping throughout the temple. The temple walls hold the eruption only because of the goodness and perfection of the architect. But within the walls, the entire structure, interior, and eminence of the temple is thrown into complete havoc. Chaos replaces beauty. Everything is scattered into disarray. The task of worship is replaced by the distraction of discord. The beauty and the mission of the temple is stripped and almost lost.

Such a loss! Such a terrible forfeiture of greatness! How could someone allow such a horror?

If we understand this story, then we can begin to grasp the sheer shock and dismay resulting from the original sin of our first parents and the Fall from grace upon human nature. The destructive results of pride; the betrayal and rebellion of sin. Human nature, so blessed and adorned with original holiness and justice, now thrown into disorientation and bewilderment. Sanctifying grace is lost. The preternatural gifts are taken away. Confusion, concupiscence, and death are unleashed to wreak havoc through our nature. This is the Fall. This is the beautiful temple almost shattered beyond recognition. This is the grenade of sin. This is the ungrateful, distressing sin of our first parents in response to the loving kindness of our Heavenly Father.

If we seek to grow in the supernatural life, and desire to comprehend why ascetical theology is imperative for a growth in holiness, then we must understand the Fall from grace and its tragic consequences. It's by knowing the loss of sanctifying grace that we can fully appreciate the gift of supernatural life.

> This entire harmony of original justice, foreseen for man in God's plan, will be lost by the sin of our first parents. (CCC 379)

LOVE AND FREEDOM

Oftentimes when people first hear about the original justice of our human nature, they have the understandable question: If our first parents had sanctifying grace and the preternatural gifts, how did they sin?

Although Adam and Eve had sanctifying grace, infused knowledge, integrity of the passions, and an immortality of the body, they were still free. In fact, their freedom was even more perfected than ours. Our first parents were free. Such freedom was a gift from God, so that they were able to truly love. It is only in being free that a person can truly love, since love requires a decision to seek the good of another, an act of the will to die to oneself for the sake of that good, and to reciprocate generously the love of another (cf. Gal 5:1,13; 1 Cor 13; 2 Cor 3:17; 1 Pet 2:16; 1 Jn 3:16).

This freedom is expressed in the figurative language of the Book of Genesis. We are told that after God formed Adam and placed him in the Garden of Eden, he explained to our first earthly father what was expected of him (and Eve). God gave him free rein over almost all of the trees of the garden. He told Adam that he could "freely eat of every tree" (2:16). God, however, told Adam (and Eve) there was one tree that was not permitted for their use. The fruit of the "Tree of the Knowledge of Good and Evil" was not to be eaten by human beings (2:17). In placing such a tree in the garden, God was giving our first parents freedom. There was a choice. As free persons, they had the power to obey, to decide to trust God their Father, and to choose what was good and true over what was evil and false.

Adam and Eve were free. Even with the gifts of original holiness and justice, they had the capacity to sin. While still possible, it was harder for them to sin. It required a more active and intentional decision. They were free, however, and had the decision before them whether to love God or rebel against him.

> Although set by God in a state of rectitude, man, enticed by the evil one, abused his freedom at the very start of history. He lifted himself up against God and sought to attain his goal apart from him. (CCC 415)

FIGURATIVE LANGUAGE

Humanity's Fall from grace is far deeper and much more intricate than the simplistic account that we often see in popular children's Bibles. In such presentations, we hear of a talking snake convincing a naked woman to eat a piece of fruit. Such a rendering might have its place in the initial Christian formation of children, but mature Christians require a deeper exploration, especially in the teachings on the supernatural life.

The account of the Fall in Genesis 3 uses figurative language. It's being used since it was the narrative genre at the time when the story was composed and redacted. What is more significant, however, is that the actual event could not be fully described in human words or stories. Figurative language is immensely helpful when there is a profundity for which human words are insufficient. The use of symbols, signs, images, emblems, and allegories comes to the aid of the human mind in narrating or speaking about events that have occurred or been experienced but are beyond literal description or summary.

In approaching the figurative language of Genesis 3—talking serpents, naked people, pieces of fruit, and all—we cannot throw out the narrative as mere "myth" and presume that this portion of the inspired Word of God lacks any truth surrounding the event that is being figuratively described. Rather, we take the historical setting of Adam and Eve and seek to understand the inner message of the language that is given to us. We approach the Word of God with reverence, kneel before it in prayer, apply the different fields of research relating to it, and explore the truths and meaning that are being expressed within it. The truth is there, contained, hidden, and recounted in a beautiful genre that goes beyond literal expression. In order to receive its truths, the sacred narrative must be prayerfully meditated upon, dissected, and then expressed in the Church's theological language for greater comprehension and understanding by the people of God.

> The account of the fall in *Genesis* 3 uses figurative language, but affirms a primeval event, a deed that took place *at the beginning of the history of man.* Revelation gives us the certainty of faith that the whole of human history is marked by the original fault freely committed by our first parents. (CCC 390)

With the clarification of figurative language in mind, we can now look at the account of the Fall from grace in Genesis 3. The narrative describes the worst event in human history. It is the event from which all other evils have come. It is the reason for the dolorous Passion and Death of the Lord Jesus Christ. It is an account steeped in signs and symbols as it describes the most horrific supernatural cataclysmic event known to humanity. Understandably, human language fails and cannot fully explain what happened in this most dreadful of events.

Let's look at the sacred narrative and see what we can learn.

THE EVIL ONE

The angel Lucifer, "full of wisdom and perfect in beauty," rebelled against God and took his minions with him to hell (cf. Lk 10:18; Rev 12:4,7–9; 2 Pet 2:4). Known as "Satan," a word meaning "Adversary," and the "Devil," a word meaning "Accuser," he sought to perpetuate his revolt against God and entered the Garden of Eden.

> Scripture speaks of a sin of these angels. This "fall" consists in the free choice of these created spirits, who radically and irrevocably *rejected* God and his reign. We find a reflection of that rebellion in the tempter's words to our first parents: "You will be like God." The devil "has sinned from the beginning"; he is "a liar and the father of lies." (*CCC* 392)

The Evil One came into the garden as an enemy to humanity. He is described as a "serpent" who is "more crafty" than all the other animals (Gen 3:1). The word "serpent" can be deceptive. Oftentimes transliterated into "snake" in popular stories, the word could actually be describing something far worse. In the Book of

34

Revelation, we are told: "The great dragon was thrown down, that ancient serpent, who is called the Devil and Satan, the deceiver of the whole world—he was thrown down to the earth, and his angels were thrown down with him" (12:9).

This suggests that the "serpent," the infamous "talking snake" in popular accounts, was actually a fierce dragon-like creature.

Of course, this is figurative language. It is describing in a physical form the wicked, disfigured, and warped existence of the Evil One. The narrative is developing the trepidation and anxiety that his presence would have provoked within our first parents. The account is significant since we are not talking about a cute garden snake, but a figuratively chronicled beast of some magnitude and malformation. Here are some other symbolic biblical accounts of the Evil One.

How you are fallen from heaven, O Day Star, son of Dawn! How you are cut down to the ground, you who laid the nations low! You said in your heart, "I will ascend to heaven; I will raise my throne above the stars of God; I will sit on the mount of assembly on the heights of Zaphon; I will ascend to the tops of the clouds, I will make myself like the Most High." (Is 14:12–14)

With an anointed cherub as guardian I placed you; you were on the holy mountain of God; you walked among the stones of fire. You were blameless in your ways from the day that you were created, until iniquity was found in you. In the abundance of your trade you were filled with violence, and you sinned; so I cast you as a profane thing from the mountain of God, and the guardian cherub drove you out from among the stones of fire. Your heart was proud because of your beauty; you corrupted your wisdom for the sake of your splendor. I cast you to the ground; I exposed you before kings, to feast their eyes on you. By the multitude of your iniquities, in the unrighteousness of your trade, you profaned your sanctuaries. So I brought out fire from within you; it consumed you, and I turned you to ashes on the earth in the sight of all who saw you. (Ezek 28:14–18)

And war broke out in heaven; Michael and his angels fought against the dragon. The dragon and his angels fought back, but they were defeated, and there was no longer any place for them in heaven. The great dragon was thrown down, that ancient serpent, who is called the Devil and Satan, the deceiver of the whole world—he was thrown down to the earth, and his angels were thrown down with him. (Rev 12:7–9)

The evil, dragon-like creature is what entered the Garden of Eden. It was the figurative representation of the Evil One who spoke to our first parents and led them into deception and their own rebellion against God.

Behind the disobedient choice of our first parents lurks a seductive voice, opposed to God, which makes them fall into death out of envy. Scripture and the Church's Tradition see in this being a fallen angel, called "Satan" or the "devil." The Church teaches that Satan was at first a good angel, made by God: "The devil and the other demons were indeed created naturally good by God, but they became evil by their own doing." (CCC 391)

THE FALL FROM GRACE

Having touched on the broader story that involves a fallen angel and our first parents, we can now look into the biblical account of humanity's Fall from grace.

In the Book of Genesis, we are told that God gave Adam the explanation of life in the Garden of Eden, with its blessings and its prohibition (2:16–17). In this way, he was the mediator of a covenant between himself (and his posterity) and the living God. Adam communicated such a way of life to Eve, as she is shown to have knowledge of it (3:2–3). She was his equal in dignity and shared in his responsibility of the covenant.

When the Evil One, "that ancient serpent," entered the garden, he did not go to the mediator of the covenant. He did not address Adam, but spoke to Eve. In the sacred narrative, the words of the Evil One are in the plural, meaning Adam and Eve were together. The narrative indicates this shared company in a more explicit way when it reads: "she took of its fruit and ate; and she also gave some to her husband, *who was with her*, and he ate" (3:6b; italics added). Although together, Eve did not defer to Adam, either as the holder of the covenant or as her husband and partner in the work of God. Eve chose to address the serpent on his terms and on her own. It was an intentional act and the regrettable set up for a terrible sin.

As the Evil One and Eve were speaking—an angel and a virgin—the use of reason was paramount. Lucifer knew that such a tactic was necessary since—due to the gift of original justice—reason controlled the passions of Eve and Adam. There was no inclination to evil, or to its lies and empty promises. And so, the Evil One approached and asked a question: "Did God

say, 'You shall not eat from any tree in the garden'?"
(3:1). He was appealing to her reason. He asked a sham
question. He knew the answer, but he wanted to start
a conversation with Eve. This is the way with evil. It
clouds truth, asks false questions, and seeks to engage
others in its darkness.

Although Eve should have banished the serpent from
her presence, our first mother's response to him was
strong and unequivocal: "We may eat of the fruit of
the trees in the garden; but God said, 'You shall not
eat of the fruit of the tree that is in the middle of the
garden, nor shall you touch it, or you shall die'" (3:2–3).
The answer was reasonable and concise. Eve knew the
blessings and prohibition of our heavenly Father. She
was close to God and began by clarifying his teachings
and moral law.

Although corrected, the Evil One had Eve exactly
where he wanted her. He turned up the pressure and
asserted: "You will not die; for God knows that when
you eat of it your eyes will be opened, and you will
be like God, knowing good and evil" (3:4b–5). Lucifer
knew that he could not appeal to Eve's passions. He
had to vanquish her through reason and the higher
functions of her spiritual soul. He lied and presented
deception as truth. He challenged the honesty of God.
He manipulated truth, saying that God was keeping
something good from Eve and Adam. He sought to
replace certainty with confusion in the soul of our first
mother. He was outright tempting Eve, through her
reason, and calling her to distrust God and reject what
God had commanded.

Eve succumbed. Rather than denounce the lies, or
declare her trust in the living God, she listened to the

foul words of the Evil One. Her soul became prey. And only after her spiritual soul caved to the whims of Lucifer, did her passions follow suit: "So when the woman saw that the tree was good for food, and that it was a delight to the eyes, and that the tree was to be desired to make one wise, she took of its fruit and ate" (3:6a). The tree then appeared appetizing and its fruit delightful. Eve thereupon disobeyed God and ate of the fruit. Next, she shared the fruit with her husband, who was equally deluded, equally disobedient, and equally guilty (3:6b).

In this singular horrific act, in which reason and passions were tragically united, the first sin is committed against the all-loving, all-holy, and ever-living God, the God whose kindness and benevolence knows no bounds.

> But I am afraid that as the serpent deceived Eve by its cunning, your thoughts will be led astray from a sincere and pure devotion to Christ. (2 Cor 11:3)

In the above account from the Book of Genesis, we receive a symbolic narrative describing the trickery and dread of the first sin. The language is as helpful as it is provocative. It points to many truths that must be discerned and understood by the posterity of Adam and Eve.

Deciphering and discerning the figurative language of the sacred narrative helps us to understand the offense given by our first parents to God our Father. The account describes not only the internal process of our first mother, but describes the hubris, the raw pride, of Adam and Eve. They allowed trust to die in their hearts. They abused their freedom, the very gift given to them by God so that they could love. A spiritual power that was meant for self-donation was manipulated and became a means for self-absorption. Our first parents thought they knew better than God, as they violated his command. They presumed he was keeping something good from them. They distrusted him and permitted suspicion to fill their hearts as they broke faith with him. The sin of Adam and Eve was an unimaginable act of defiance and delinquency. An all-loving God had blessed them with existence and kindness, and they reciprocated with nothing except obstinacy and hostility.

Realized within the figurative language of the Book of Genesis, we can see the pernicious and vile sin of our first parents.

> In that sin man *preferred* himself to God and by that very act scorned him. He chose himself over and against God, against the requirements of his creaturely status and therefore against his own good. Constituted in a state of holiness, man was destined to be fully "divinized" by God in glory. Seduced by the devil, he wanted to "be like God," but "without God, before God, and not in accordance with God." (CCC 398)

DEATH AND THE
"KNOWLEDGE OF GOOD AND EVIL"

In dissecting the sacred narrative, we need to understand the nature of the Evil One's argument. What was being posed to our first parents?

First, the Evil One dismissed the sentence for breaking God's command. He told Eve, "You will not die"

(3:4b). Lucifer challenged the truthfulness of God and his justice. At this point, our first parents still shared in immortality. Through the preternatural gifts, their bodies shared in the immortality of their souls. If they broke their bond with God, these gifts would be lost. They would, in truth, die. Adam and Eve trusted God and obeyed, until the Evil One began to spread confusion and doubt.

When Lucifer told our first mother, "you will not die," he was telling her that she could not trust God. She and Adam could have the abundance of life without God. Furthermore, they could share immortality without the all-living and everlasting God. They could be his equal, or even his superior. It was a seductive invitation to full rebellion, a tactic that was well-known to the Evil One.

What should we make of the actual temptation: to have knowledge of good and evil? Is this an evil thing? Didn't our first parents already have such a knowledge, namely, eat of all these trees, but not of this one?

Certainly, Adam and Eve had a general awareness of good and evil. They needed such knowledge to exercise their freedom and to love. The temptation, therefore, was located within the mind of our first parents. It was posed to their spiritual souls. The temptation was not a broad knowledge of good and evil, but rather the power to determine for themselves what was good and what was evil. Adam and Eve—not God—would decide what was morally acceptable and what was not. It was rebellion. It was a cold attempt to usurp divine authority and to steal what our human faculties could never fully use and what properly belongs to God.

With this imagery, Revelation teaches that *the power to decide what is good and what is evil does not belong to man, but to God alone.* The man is certainly free, inasmuch as he can understand and accept God's commands. And he possesses an extremely far-reaching freedom, since he can eat "of every tree of the garden." But his freedom is not unlimited: it must halt before the "tree of the knowledge of good and evil," for it is called to accept the moral law given by God. In fact, human freedom finds its authentic and complete fulfilment precisely in the acceptance of that law. God, who alone is good, knows perfectly what is good for man, and by virtue of his very love proposes this good to man in the commandments. (John Paul II, *Veritatis Splendor*, 35)

This sly, internal move of mind and heart is the first sin. Adam and Eve sought to steal the divine majesty for themselves, to remove God, and to become gods themselves in their own right. It was pride. It was a revolt against God. It was a carrying of a grenade into the beautiful temple of our human nature. Such an insurrection would have consequences. God will lovingly show his mercy and justice to our first parents.

God created man in his image and established him in his friendship. A spiritual creature, man can live this friendship only in free submission to God. The prohibition against eating "of the tree of the knowledge of good and evil" spells this out: "for in the day that you eat of it, you shall die." The "tree of the

42

knowledge of good and evil" symbolically evokes the insurmountable limits that man, being a creature, must freely recognize and respect with trust. Man is dependent on his Creator, and subject to the laws of creation and to the moral norms that govern the use of freedom. (CCC 396)

CONSEQUENCES OF THE FALL

The biblical narrative continues to describe the interaction between God and our first parents, our first parents themselves, the relationship between them, and their interaction with the world around them. In each case, God sought to give blessings of harmony and peace. Now, due to the tragedy of sin, tension and discord will mark these relationships.

In the first sin, Adam and Eve, human nature, and creation itself all suffered a drastic fall. The grenade went off and the temple, and everything connected with it, was thrown into chaos.

Immediately after the first sin, sanctifying grace and the preternatural gifts were lost. Humanity's natural state was left to its own powers. Human nature without divine grace. Human nature without the help of the preternatural gifts. It was wounded and in shock. It now lacked a proper balance within itself and was disoriented by the immense loss it had suffered.

The Book of Genesis figurately explains: "Then the eyes of both were opened, and they knew that they were naked; and they sewed fig leaves together and made loincloths for themselves" (3:7).

By his sin Adam, as the first man, lost the original holiness and justice he had received from God, not only for himself but for all human beings. (CCC 416)

The most utterly shocking consequence of all was the loss of sanctifying grace to human nature. The intimate relationship humanity was to have with God our Father was severed and broken. The children of God became orphans. God appeared to be a stranger and a threat. To this day he seems removed from us. Caricatures are created about him and he is kept at bay. We cannot accurately know him without his grace. We cannot walk with him in the breeze of the evening.

The Book of Genesis tells us:

They heard the sound of the LORD God walking in the garden at the time of the evening breeze, and the man and his wife hid themselves from the presence of the LORD God among the trees of the garden. But the LORD God called to the man, and said to him, "Where are you?" He said, "I heard the sound of you in the garden, and I was afraid, because I was naked; and I hid myself." He said, "Who told you that you were naked? Have you eaten from the tree of which I commanded you not to eat?" (Gen 3:8–11)

Scripture portrays the tragic consequences of this first disobedience. Adam and Eve immediately lose the grace of original holiness. They become afraid of the God of whom they have conceived a distorted image— that of a God jealous of his prerogatives. (CCC 399)

The preternatural gifts of infused knowledge, integrity of the passions, and the immortality of the body are also taken from our human nature.

The Book of Genesis recounts the discipline of God upon Adam and Eve, our human nature, and upon creation.

Adam did not take responsibility. He dismissed his role as husband and holder of the covenant with God. He blamed Eve: "The man said, 'The woman whom you gave to be with me, she gave me fruit from the tree, and I ate'" (3:12). The marital relationship was to be one of mutual love and deference, service and kindly support. With the Fall, it now becomes marked by blame, battles for power, and selfishness. As with the marital union, so with all other human relationships. Neighbors are viewed with suspicion and jealousy, rather than magnanimity and kindness.

In her turn, Eve also deflected responsibility and blamed the serpent: "The woman said, 'The serpent tricked me, and I ate'" (3:13b). In this action, Eve denounced the serpent, which she should have done during his temptation earlier.

In either case, our first parents did not acknowledge their sin or repent. They did not ask for mercy. They were only concerned about themselves and their own justification. They forgot about their bond with God and each other. The first sin has already taken its toll as such self-centeredness becomes the rule of the day in the heart and actions of Adam and Eve.

> You have never heard, you have never known, from of old your ear has not been opened. For I knew that you would deal very treacherously, and that from birth you were called a rebel. (Is 48:8)

45

As a loving Father, God brings discipline to his children. The removal of the preternatural gifts can be gleaned from the sacred narrative.

The integrity of the passions is lost. They now wage war against reason, and reason itself becomes wayward and inclined to error. Our internal harmony is now severed. Our souls are filled with stress and agitation. We are subject to concupiscence, meaning we are inclined to evil and easy prey to its allure and empty promises. As a sign of this loss within our human nature, God showed Eve its consequences in her relationship with Adam: "I will greatly increase your pangs in childbearing; in pain you shall bring forth children, yet your desire shall be for your husband, and he shall rule over you" (3:16).

> I do not understand my own actions. For I do not do what I want, but I do the very thing I hate. (Rom 7:15)

The gift of infused knowledge is also removed from our nature. No longer will knowledge be immediately given and remembered. Now, we must struggle to learn, be educated by pain, and labor to remember what we have been taught. As a reflection of this loss, God tells Adam that he will toil the earth but not have the skills for, or successes of, such work: "Because you have listened to the voice of your wife, and have eaten of the tree about which I commanded you, 'You shall not eat of it,' cursed is the ground because of you; in toil you shall eat of it all the days of your life; thorns and thistles it shall bring forth for you; and you shall eat the plants of the field" (3:17–18).

> They are darkened in their understanding, alienated
> from the life of God because of their ignorance and
> hardness of heart. (Eph 4:18)

The immortality of the body is also removed from
our human nature. The body now becomes corruptible.
It will suffer, become sick, and die. God did not desire
death for his children, but our first parents presumed
to know more than he does. By sin, death entered the
world. God tells Adam: "By the sweat of your face you
shall eat bread until you return to the ground, for out
of it you were taken; you are dust, and to dust you
shall return" (3:19).

> Therefore, just as sin came into the world through
> one man, and death came through sin, and so death
> spread to all because all have sinned... (Rom 5:12)

Original holiness and justice were lost. Sin brought
terrible consequences and God the Father exercised
discipline toward his children. What a horrible loss
for the human race! Now, God appears as a stranger
and the preternatural helps to our human nature are
gone. The chaos and debris of our nature is left. The
pieces are thrown everywhere. Our nature is wounded
and perplexed.

> The harmony in which they had found themselves,
> thanks to original justice, is now destroyed: the
> control of the soul's spiritual faculties over the

body is shattered; the union of man and woman becomes subject to tensions, their relations henceforth marked by lust and domination. Harmony with creation is broken: visible creation has become alien and hostile to man. Because of man, creation is now subject "to its bondage to decay." Finally, the consequence explicitly foretold for this disobedience will come true: man will "return to the ground," for out of it he was taken. *Death makes its entrance into human history.* (CCC 400)

ORIGINAL SIN

As sharers in human nature, every human person suffers from the loss of our first parents. Each of us is born with original sin. Sanctifying grace is suspended, and we do not receive it immediately at conception or birth. None of us receives the preternatural gifts. We are given life with original sin.

Your first ancestor sinned, and your interpreters transgressed against me. (Is 43:27)

How can the sin of Adam and Eve bear consequences for us? The question requires us to consider the uniqueness of their original status and their place as the head of our nature. We are united in one body with Adam and Eve. We all hold the same nature. We are all bound to each other.

Admittedly, however, the passing on of original sin is a mystery that cannot be understood in its own right.

Only later with the coming of the Redeemer will the collective condition of our nature and its shared consequences (and blessings) come to light.

> Only the light of divine Revelation clarifies the reality of sin and particularly of the sin committed at mankind's origins. Without the knowledge Revelation gives of God we cannot recognize sin clearly and are tempted to explain it as merely a developmental flaw, a psychological weakness, a mistake, or the necessary consequence of an inadequate social structure, etc. Only in the knowledge of God's plan for man can we grasp that sin is an abuse of the freedom that God gives to created persons so that they are capable of loving him and loving one another. (*CCC* 387)

Adam and Eve received the gifts of original holiness and justice for the whole of the human race, and not only for themselves. By sinning, our first parents committed a personal sin, but as the head of our human nature, their personal sin affected human nature itself. And so, human nature fell with the sin of our first parents.

Every human person after Adam and Eve, therefore, receives a fallen human nature. As members of the human family, we continue to share in the Fall. Our nature is now deprived of original holiness and justice. This is what is meant by original sin. And so, this is why original sin "is called 'sin' only in an analogical sense: it is a sin 'contracted' and not 'committed'—a state and not an act" (*CCC* 404).

Indeed, I was born guilty, a sinner when my mother conceived me. (Ps 51:5)

Although every human person save one has original sin, it is not a personal sin and does not carry personal guilt. It is a deprivation of original holiness and justice. While wounded, our human nature is not totally corrupted. Our human nature is wounded in its natural powers and is now subject to ignorance, suffering, and the dominion of death. There is also an inclination to sin.

In this way, original sin is the disgraceful foundation of all other evil. Its shameful legacy can be seen in the habit of sin seen throughout human history.

The doctrine of original sin, closely connected with that of redemption by Christ, provides lucid discernment of man's situation and activity in the world. By our first parents' sin, the devil has acquired a certain domination over man, even though man remains free. Original sin entails "captivity under the power of him who thenceforth had the power of death, that is, the devil." Ignorance of the fact that man has a wounded nature inclined to evil gives rise to serious errors in the areas of education, politics, social action, and morals. (CCC 407)

The conclusion of the account of the Fall, however, cannot be forgotten. Even as he exercises discipline toward his children, God shows his love and gentle kindness to Adam and Eve: "And the LORD God made garments of skins for the man and for his wife, and clothed them" (3:21). In the figurative language of Genesis, we are told that God still loves his children, will still care for them, and desires them to be with him. As a sign of this love, God also gave them a promise of a wounded savior: "I will put enmity between you and the woman, and between your offspring and hers; he will strike your head, and you will strike his heel" (3:15). The wounded savior will come, and he will bring redemption with him.

> But when the fullness of time had come, God sent his Son, born of a woman, born under the law, in order to redeem those who were under the law, so that we might receive adoption as children. (Gal 4:4–5)

APPLICATION: TAKING IT TO HEART

Having explored the Fall from grace, it's now important for us to apply this awareness to the ascetical life and see how it can help us to grow in our supernatural life with God.

The following spiritual exercises are suggested as helps in the work of the ascetical life.

Focus from the Holy Mass

Reflect upon the *Sanctus, Sanctus, Sanctus* prayer of the Mass: "Holy, Holy, Holy Lord God of hosts. Heaven and earth are full of your glory. Hosanna in the highest. Blessed is he who comes in the name of the Lord. Hosanna in the highest."

Consider: 1) The utter, all-holiness of God; 2) God's sheer goodness and his love for us; 3) The desire of God to ransom us from our sins. The word "hosanna" is a messianic acclamation that means, "save, we beg." Allow your heart to experience a crying out for redemption.

Lectio Divina *Suggestion*

Spend some time, perhaps five to fifteen minutes, repeating and breathing into your heart the following portion of the living Word of God: "He said to them, 'I watched Satan fall from heaven like a flash of lightning. See, I have given you authority to tread on snakes and scorpions, and over all the power of the enemy; and nothing will hurt you'" (Lk 10:18–19).

Consider: The Second Person of the Holy Trinity witnessing the foul practice and deception of the Evil One. God the Son watching Lucifer being thrown from heaven. Grieve over his deception of our first parents. Reflect upon Lucifer. Call him a murderer and a liar. Denounce him. Declare God your Father and make a strong act of faith in him alone. Ask the Lord Jesus to heal you with his grace.

Meditation Theme

Use your spiritual imagination and compose a place. Imagine the sights, smells, sounds, taste, and touch of the environment. Allow yourself to be truly, spiritually present in that moment.

Compose the exchange between the Evil One and our first parents. Imagine the harmony within the hearts of our first parents, like music playing throughout their souls. Hear the music. Feel the confidence. Imagine their inner peace and the tranquility between them. See Adam and Eve smile at each other. Reflect upon their shared glances and playfulness. Consider a world without suffering or death. Peruse the Garden of Eden. Look upon the Tree of the Knowledge of Good and Evil. Compare and contrast it with the other trees. When the time is right, begin your colloquy, your conversation with God. Ask him the questions on your heart. Listen quietly. Love deeply. Know that God is with you.

Poustinia Meditation

This method is different from other forms of prayer. The task is to clear your mind of all thoughts and attempt to think of nothing other than a simple word. It can be repeated multiple times or simply held in our minds. Sometimes the use of a foreign word can help us stay focused. For our exercise today, focus on the word: "Peccare" (Latin for "to sin"), or another word that has stood out to you during this chapter.

Examination of Conscience

Do I purposely place myself in occasions of sin?
Have I failed to respect the authority of others?
Do I dialogue with darkness?
Have I sought to justify or rationalize my sins?
Have I led others into sin with me?
Have I reflected upon the total horror of original sin?
Do I consider our inclination to sin when deciding
    what entertainment to watch?
Do I dabble with sorcery or superstition?
Have I lied to protect myself from discipline?
Have I failed to repent properly of my sins?

Suggested Saints and Holy Ones

In the early Church, Saint Paul was one of the most preeminent rabbis. He knew the theology of the Old Testament and studied the words and deeds of God. He knew the tragedy of original sin and lamented its consequences in his own life. He bemoaned the fallenness of his own soul as he did the evil he despised and failed to do the good he wanted to do. He saw the same fallenness in others and called for conversion and reform throughout his apostolic ministry.

As we seek holiness, and the internal peace that comes with it, we can turn to this father in the faith and ask for his prayers and spiritual mentoring.

> The saying is sure and worthy of full acceptance, that Christ Jesus came into the world to save sinners—of whom I am the foremost. But for that very reason I received mercy, so that in me, as the foremost, Jesus Christ might display the utmost patience, making me an example to those who would come to believe in him for eternal life. (1 Tim 1:15-16)

Three Prayers from Our Tradition

ACT OF LOVE

O my God,
I love you above all things,
with my whole heart and soul,
because you are all-good and worthy of all love.
I love my neighbor as myself for the love of you.
I forgive all who have injured me,
and ask pardon of all whom I have injured. *Amen.*

BREASTPLATE OF SAINT PATRICK

Christ be with me, Christ within me,
Christ behind me, Christ before me,
Christ beside me, Christ to win me,
Christ to comfort and restore me.
Christ beneath me, Christ above me,
Christ in quiet, Christ in danger,
Christ in hearts of all that love me,
Christ in mouth of friend and stranger.
Amen.

GUARDIAN ANGEL PRAYER

Angel of God,
my guardian dear,
To whom God's love
commits me here,
Ever this day,
be at my side,
To light and guard,
To rule and guide.
Amen.

CHAPTER THREE

Our Redemption in Jesus Christ

For God so loved the world that he gave his only
Son, so that everyone who believes in him may
not perish but may have eternal life.

John 3:16

AN OLDER BROTHER'S LOVE

SOME TIME AGO, DURING A PASTO-ral visit in a hospital, I spoke with a man who shared with me that he could never understand why Jesus Christ would suffer for him and how he could take away his sins. The man explained that he used this line of reasoning as a defense against the claims of the Lord Jesus and his Church.

The bastion broke, however, when his older brother died. As he grieved his brother's loss, the man was reminded of his older brother's care for him. The older sibling would take the blame for his younger brother, go the extra mile to help him, and offer numerous sacrifices that helped the younger sibling to receive opportunities and blessings.

Only in reliving his brother's life of love and service could the man begin to understand why Jesus Christ

56

would suffer for him and how he could remove his sins. In placing the Lord Jesus within the context of Older Brother, the man could begin to see. Scales fell from his eyes. He began to see Jesus Christ as if for the first time and began to realize what the Lord did for him and all humanity.

It was precisely this awakening that allowed the man to accept the unconditional love of God, repent of his sins, and open his heart to the Lord Jesus and the workings of his grace. In telling me his story, the man recounted the freedom and peace that come with the hope of salvation in Jesus Christ.

Do we understand what Jesus Christ has done for us? Do we realize the gift of salvation that is offered to us by God?

The redemption of the human family has come through a sacrificial act of love by God the Son. This act reveals to us the concurrent movements of God the Father and God the Holy Spirit. Each of the Persons of the Holy Trinity is involved: God the Son offering the sacrifice, God the Father ratifying it, and God the Holy Spirit fulfilling it. Redemption is accomplished for the sake of our salvation. Redemption is completed so that we might be children of God.

Our redemption powerfully unveils to us the immensity of God's love for us. It is a masterpiece of God's love! It is the entrance and the source of our sharing in God's divine nature. It is the mystery at the heart of the supernatural life and the mystery by which we know God and can be in a familial relationship with him.

It is essential for our own growth in the supernatural life that we diligently seek to understand the mystery of our redemption in Jesus Christ.

> For the one who sanctifies and those who are sanctified all have one Father. For this reason Jesus is not ashamed to call them brothers and sisters. (Heb 2:11)
>
> For you did not receive a spirit of slavery to fall back into fear, but you have received a spirit of adoption. When we cry, "Abba! Father!" it is that very Spirit bearing witness with our spirit that we are children of God, and if children, then heirs, heirs of God and joint heirs with Christ—if, in fact, we suffer with him so that we may also be glorified with him. (Rom 8:15–17)

THE PROTOEVANGELIUM

In order for us to fully understand the mystery of our redemption, we have to return to the promise given to our first parents after the Fall from grace.

After the Fall, God the Father allowed certain disciplines to befall the human race. He did not, however, leave us to our own devices or deprive us of hope. In spite of humanity's betrayal, God the Father showed us his love and promised us a savior. The Evil One would be vanquished. Sin and death—consequences of the Fall—would be destroyed. Humanity would once again share in the life of God and confidently call him "Father."

The figurative language of the Book of Genesis gives us an account of this promise.

> I will put enmity between you and the woman, and between your offspring and hers; he will strike your head, and you will strike his heel. (Gen 3:15)

The passage is so uniquely consumed with hope that the Christian Tradition has always revered it as the

Protoevangelium, namely, the "first gospel." It is the first indication of the Good News that will come later in Jesus Christ.

In order for us to understand the Good News, we have to dissect the sacred narrative. In doing so, we discover some significant details:

▸ The woman and the Evil One were in conversation, which led to the Fall of our first parents. The two, therefore, are held accountable. From the two of them, there is posterity of sorts. The woman will have children from her womb. Lucifer has his minions, a dark type of children. There will be enmity between the children of the one and the children of the other. They will be at war.

▸ The promise moves from a plural description to one of singularity. From the woman's posterity, a son will arise. He will strike the head of the serpent. He will be mighty, therefore, and of great strength. As revealed later in salvation history, he will have a divine anointing upon him. He will be the Messiah, a Hebrew word for "anointed one." He will be Christ, a Greek word also meaning "anointed one." He will crush the power of the Evil One. He will be true redeemer and lasting savior of God's people.

▸ The passage also moves from the plural to the singular as it refocuses on Lucifer. Although he will be crushed, the Evil One will strike the heel of the savior. He will cause harm. The savior, therefore, will be wounded and endure pain. In the Messiah of God, suffering will be the path to our redemption.

▸ In the biblical account, we see the battle that will happen between the Messiah of God and the Evil One. We are told of his victory, but also of his wounds. The promise is the inheritance of God's people and the basis of salvation history as God prepares his people for its fulfillment.

In the fullness of time, this promise will come to completion in Jesus of Nazareth, true God and true man. The Messiah—the Christ—is God himself. This is an unimaginable mystery—completely unexpected. What a beautiful love God has for his people! He himself becomes our Redeemer and our Savior. He himself will ransom us. He himself will undergo suffering. God-Incarnate will vanquish evil and darkness from the inside out. He will conquer death by undergoing its pains. This is the account of our redemption in Jesus Christ.

As best we can, we must explore and seek to understand this saving mystery.

> After his fall, man was not abandoned by God. On the contrary, God calls him and in a mysterious way heralds the coming victory over evil and his restoration from his fall. This passage in Genesis is called the *Protoevangelium* ("first gospel"): the first announcement of the Messiah and Redeemer, of a battle between the serpent and the Woman, and of the final victory of a descendant of hers. (CCC 410)

SAVED BY HOPE

The rebellion of our first parents merited consequences. In response, God the Father could have wiped out humanity and creation. It would have been just. God could also have suspended his special providence and left creation and young humanity to its own devices. It would have been just. And yet, God did not choose active vengeance nor passive vengeance. Instead, he showed the willingness of his love to be with his children. In light of the blatant offense, he gave a tempered discipline. In the midst of the discipline, he also gave the promise of a savior.

If our first parents had been left to suffer the consequences of the Fall without such a promise, they would certainly have fallen into despair. They knew what had been given to them and what had been lost. It was overwhelming. The promise of a savior, of restoration, of redemption was their sole cause for hope.

The hope that is born from this singularly powerful promise is at the heart of the relationship between God and his people. It gives birth to a profound longing and pining for salvation in him. The hope this breeds is beyond anything offered by this fallen and passing world. It is a hope that reminds us of what hope truly is, namely, a complete reliance on God and the anticipation of fellowship with him here and into eternity.

> Hope is the theological virtue by which we desire the kingdom of heaven and eternal life as our happiness, placing our trust in Christ's promises and relying not on our own strength, but on the help of the grace of the Holy Spirit. (*CCC* 1817)

True hope, therefore, is not a trust in our own powers or abilities to change things or to make them into what we want them to be. Such an understanding of hope is similar to that of the Greek mindset and the pagan worldview. False hope perpetuates our human anguish since it claims that our human spirit has a power to control or change things, when it does not. False hope constrains us to a perpetual cycle of disappointment and failure.

An explanation of this fallen hope can be seen in the pagan myth about Pandora's Box. In the story, Zeus presents Pandora with a gift. As she opens the box, death, suffering, sickness, and all the evils of the world pour out upon humanity. At the bottom of the box was hope. According to the myth, hope was the worst curse of all. It was a hubris that convinced humanity that it could handle the horrors unleashed upon it. There was no help from the gods, and no power within humanity to address the injuries inflicted upon it, and so any hope was a self-delusion. False hope is a self-curse.

In contrast to the pagan myth, the Book of Genesis shows us a loving Father who disciplines his children for their own good. Yes, he gives discipline to his children, but he also gives a promise of redemption. This promise gives true hope, since it is a hope in God, who does love us, wants to care for us, and orders creation according to his benevolent providence.

> Let us hold fast to the confession of our hope without wavering, for he who has promised is faithful. (Heb 10:23)

True hope, therefore, shows us our limitations and weaknesses. It calls us outside of ourselves and reveals to us the power and wisdom of God. Rather than setting us up for frustration and failure, hope directs us to seek the help of God's grace and to pine for his saving work in our world today.

> This Spirit he poured out on us richly through Jesus
> Christ our Savior, so that, having been justified by
> his grace, we might become heirs according to the
> hope of eternal life. (Tit 3:6–7)

These two versions of hope were referenced by Saint
Paul, when he wrote about the great patriarch Abraham:
"For the promise that he would inherit the world did
not come to Abraham or to his descendants through the
law but through the righteousness of faith.... Hoping
against hope, he believed that he would become 'the
father of many nations,' according to what was said, 'So
numerous shall your descendants be'" (Rom 4:13, 18).

Abraham, we are told, "hoped against hope." This
is not a literary device. The great patriarch hoped in
God, and so hoped against the false "hope" of the fallen
world. He knew that he had no power in himself. He
was weak and a suppliant before God. He, therefore,
denounced the false hope of our fallen world and hoped
in God. In this way, he actually "hoped against hope."

> For in hope we were saved. Now hope that is seen
> is not hope. For who hopes for what is seen? But
> if we hope for what we do not see, we wait for it
> with patience. (Rom 8:24–25)

This is the inheritance of those who live with the
promise of a Savior.

By recalling the promise, we are given the source
of the generation-upon-generation hope for salvation
among God's people. Each phase of salvation history,
with its own twists and turns, anguish and supplications,

reflected the primordial hope of the first promise. The promise was the thin line that ran all through God's words and deeds, as he molded and shaped his people to receive the Messiah.

In the fullness of time, God fulfilled this promise in his Son, Jesus Christ. In Christ, the hope of salvation is given. Humanity has received its Savior. Now, the task of every person is to share in the exercise of hope, and to turn to the Lord Jesus and seek the fulfillment of that promise in themselves. Humanity lived in hope and has received its Redeemer. Each person must live in hope and ask for the work of that redemption to be brought to him for his own salvation. We live in hope. We are saved in hope.

> I am confident of this, that the one who began a good work among you will bring it to completion by the day of Jesus Christ. (Phil 1:6)

Having hope in our hearts, let's return to the *Protoevangelium* and explore the role of the Woman in the work of our redemption.

OUR REDEEMER AND HIS MOTHER

The Fall of humanity came through a man and a woman. As such, God's harmonious providence will heal the wound by the same means as the offense. And so, a man and a woman will work together to bring about our redemption.

While the first man and woman were husband and wife, the second set of man and woman will be mother and son. Since the "Woman" of the Fall became the "mother of all living" (Gen 3:20), God places our redemption within the context of motherhood since the enmity—the battle—is for life, human and divine. And so, it is the seed of the Woman who will crush the head of the Evil One. It will be the son of the Woman who becomes our Savior and Redeemer.

The victory of the long-awaited Savior will be brought about through his mother. They are united in his saving work. The Woman—his mother—will have her part in the Father's plan of salvation.

As a virgin and an angel—Eve and Lucifer—brought about damnation to humanity by a piece of fruit, so a virgin and an angel—Mary and Gabriel—will begin humanity's redemption by the fruit of her womb. Prepared for her mission and vocation from the first moment of her immaculate conception, and the recipient of the graces of redemption in a prevenient way, Mary of Nazareth, the Woman of the promise of Genesis, served as the Savior's Mother and cooperated with him in a singular way in the work of our redemption.

Our Lady continues to fulfill her vocation as she calls us to love and trust her divine Son. Mary is our spiritual Mother and a help to us in growing in the supernatural life.

> When Jesus saw his mother and the disciple whom he loved standing beside her, he said to his mother, "Woman, here is your son." (Jn 19:26)

Grasping the full extent of different layers of the *Protoevangelium*, we can now dive into the riches of its fulfilment in Jesus Christ.

The Christian tradition sees in this passage an announcement of the "New Adam" who, because he "became obedient unto death, even death on a cross," makes amends superabundantly for the disobedience of Adam. Furthermore many Fathers and Doctors of the Church have seen the woman announced in the *"Protoevangelium"* as Mary, the mother of Christ, the "new Eve." Mary benefited first of all and uniquely from Christ's victory over sin: she was preserved from all stain of original sin and by a special grace of God committed no sin of any kind during her whole earthly life. (CCC 411)

THE WORK OF OUR REDEMPTION

At the moment of creation, God the Father foresaw the Fall. Although he did not will it, he was aware of the forthcoming betrayal of Adam and Eve. As such, his plan always included a Savior. At the appointed hour in God's divine providence, therefore, the promised Savior came to us, the dawn from on high broke upon us (Lk 1:78). God came to us as our Rescuer and Redeemer. When the Savior came to us, it was not as a removed figure falling from the sky. He did not emerge from the sea, nor was he born from the mind of his divine father, or from a peculiar sexual encounter, as was commonly said of divinities within the myths of Greece and Rome. The Son of God was not a ghost or a mere theophany. He was Savior and fully human.

Through sin and its consequences, humanity became damaged and disfigured. In the Savior, Jesus Christ, humanity is offered the possibility of being restored and remade in his likeness.

> But *why did God not prevent the first man from sinning?* St. Leo the Great responds, "Christ's inexpressible grace gave us blessings better than those the demon's envy had taken away." And St. Thomas Aquinas wrote, "There is nothing to prevent human nature's being raised up to something greater, even after sin; God permits evil in order to draw forth some greater good. Thus St. Paul says, 'Where sin increased, grace abounded all the more'; and the Exsultet sings, 'O happy fault, . . . which gained for us so great a Redeemer!'" (CCC 412)

In becoming a human being, the God-man, Jesus Christ, became the head of humanity. He became a new Adam. As Adam held headship of humanity, so the Lord Jesus. In such a position, the Lord's actions affected the whole of humanity. And so, he was able to offer expiation for our sins. He was able to offer us sanctifying grace, which is a familial, supernatural relationship with God and his divine indwelling within us. The Lord Jesus was able to open again the gates of heaven to those who seek eternity with God.

As the first Adam brought sin and death, so the New Adam—Jesus Christ—brought good from evil, salvation from damnation. He balanced justice with divine goodness.

> For since death came through a human being, the resurrection of the dead has also come through a human being; for as all die in Adam, so all will be made alive in Christ. (1 Cor 15:21–22)

As we dive into the inner workings of our redemption, we can discern that the offense of sin required: 1) a satisfactory reparation proportionate to the offense of sin, described biblically as a strike at the heel; and, 2) the reparation to be made by a lawful representative of humanity, explained biblically as the offspring of the Woman. These are the conditions by which the ancient promise of a savior will be fulfilled.

In the completion of the promise, the long-awaited Savior was the eternal Son of God, who becomes the head of humanity, and offers his suffering and death as an atonement for sin.

> Justification has been *merited for us by the Passion of Christ* who offered himself on the cross as a living victim, holy and pleasing to God, and whose blood has become the instrument of atonement for the sins of all men. (CCC 1992)

Clearly, the conditions are infinitely fulfilled.

1. The reparation offered by Jesus Christ is not only satisfactory, but it greatly surpasses the offense. The sacrifice of the Son of God is far beyond the sins of humanity. Yes, the reparation is disproportionate to the offense. Not as a deficit, but as a surplus. Truth be told, any simple act of the Son of God would have been satisfactory as a reparation for the sins of humanity. The Incarnation alone, God becoming a man, could have been a sufficient reparation. Moved by the immensity of his love for the Father and for humanity, the Lord Jesus offered innumerable acts that could

68

have been satisfactory. The entire life of the Lord was a continual, selfless sacrifice to the Father. He filled the measure that was required and then exceeded it beyond imagination. He crowned his life of sacrifice with the most glorious, exalted, and imposing sacrifice of all, namely, his complete and total immolation of himself. He will allow the Evil One, that ancient foe, to strike at his heel.

Let the same mind be in you that was in Christ Jesus, who, though he was in the form of God, did not regard equality with God as something to be exploited, but emptied himself, taking the form of a slave, being born in human likeness. And being found in human form, he humbled himself and became obedient to the point of death— even death on a cross. Therefore God also highly exalted him and gave him the name that is above every name, so that at the name of Jesus every knee should bend, in heaven and on earth and under the earth, and every tongue should confess that Jesus Christ is Lord, to the glory of God the Father. (Phil 2:5–11)

2. The Lord Jesus, as God-man, holds the headship of humanity and is, therefore, the greatest of representatives of humanity before God. He is the New Adam. He is the son of Mary, the "Woman" of the promise.

For just as by the one man's disobedience the many were made sinners, so by the one man's obedience the many will be made righteous. But law came in,

> with the result that the trespass multiplied; but
> where sin increased, grace abounded all the more,
> so that, just as sin exercised dominion in death, so
> grace might also exercise dominion through justi-
> fication leading to eternal life through Jesus Christ
> our Lord. (Rom 5:19–21)

The promise of a Savior is fulfilled. Redemption is at hand. In Jesus Christ, salvation is offered to those who seek it. Sin is absolved. Sanctifying grace is given. Heaven is made available.

> The victory that Christ won over sin has given us
> greater blessings than those which sin had taken
> from us: "where sin increased, grace abounded all
> the more." (CCC 420)

THE PRETERNATURAL GIFTS AND
THE THEOLOGICAL VIRTUES

As the Lord Jesus restored sanctifying grace to human-ity and welcomed us back into a supernatural, familial relationship with God, we might understandably have questions about the preternatural gifts.

If our original holiness is returned to us, where is the original justice of the preternatural gifts? Why have these not been restored to us?

God the Father could have restored the preternat-ural gifts, but he did not. God allows us to suffer with their loss as a help to us in cooperating with grace and working out our salvation in Jesus Christ. The loss of these gifts will be a temporal punishment of the Fall that we will carry throughout human history.

> Baptism, by imparting the life of Christ's grace, erases original sin and turns a man back toward God, but the consequences for nature, weakened and inclined to evil, persist in man and summon him to spiritual battle. (CCC 405)

God permits this suffering so that we can understand the gravity of sin, cling to the grace offered to us in Jesus Christ, actively cooperate with that grace allowing it to transform us, and labor as best we can—through the valley of tears of a fallen world—to work out our salvation in Jesus Christ. The opportunity of suffering in this life, therefore, is a call to purification and an invitation to love.

> Therefore, my beloved, just as you have always obeyed me, not only in my presence, but much more now in my absence, work out your own salvation with fear and trembling; for it is God who is at work in you, enabling you both to will and to work for his good pleasure. (Phil 2:12–13)

Though dispossessed of the preternatural gifts, we do receive a different set of supernatural gifts in Jesus Christ that surpass them in greatness. In addition to the infinite gift of sanctifying grace, we also receive the infused theological virtues of faith, hope, and charity.

These virtues are placed within our souls as we are baptized in Jesus Christ. They are an inheritance of the elect, who are chosen and reborn in the Lord Jesus. The three virtues have natural counterparts and are oftentimes confused with their natural expression. The three virtues, however, are rightly called "theological" since they pertain to God (and "God" in Greek is *theos*).

As an example, I can use natural faith to believe geologists when they tell me there is a continent called Australia. If I'm home, however, and there's a knock at the door, and when I open it, Australia is there and tells me, "Hey, I'm a continent," and I believe because Australia told me it exists, then that would be an example of how theological faith works. Theological faith believes in God because of God's own witness to himself. Similarly, theological hope trusts in God because of his goodness and trustworthiness. And, theological love truly loves God because he is lovable and is the source of all love.

> Justification is at the same time the *acceptance of God's righteousness* through faith in Jesus Christ. Righteousness (or "justice") here means the rectitude of divine love. With justification, faith, hope, and charity are poured into our hearts, and obedience to the divine will is granted us. (*CCC* 1991)

In these examples, we can see the focus is on God himself. The supernatural virtues are received and exercised only within the workings of sanctifying grace. The unbeliever cannot have such a supernatural faith, hope, and love of God. He is restricted to believe, trust, and love God on the merely natural level.

By understanding the power of these infused virtues, therefore, we can see how they are a greater inheritance than the preternatural gifts.

▶ Theological faith is stronger than infused knowledge. While not as easy as infused knowledge, supernatural faith helps us to know God himself, his revelations, and his truth.

▶ Theological hope is more robust than an immortality of body. While we will still undergo disease, illness, and death in this life, theological hope shows us the glory of heaven and guides us to seek eternal beatitude with God.

▶ Theological love is more dynamic than an integrity of the passions. Yes, we will have to fight the battle with our passions, but theological love reveals God's immense and passionate love. We can see and experience God's love. This knowledge fortifies us and helps us to order everything in our lives to God and his loving kindness.

In this way, we can see how the supernatural life is edified and lifted up by the theological virtues of faith, hope, and charity.

As we seek to grow in the supernatural life, these virtues are necessary. Each of them must be nurtured, well formed by truth, and prudently exercised in our lives. In this way, we can grow in wisdom and grace before God and humanity.

The human virtues are rooted in the theological virtues, which adapt man's faculties for participation in the divine nature: for the theological virtues relate directly to God. They dispose Christians to live in a relationship with the Holy Trinity. They have the One and Triune God for their origin, motive, and object.

The theological virtues are the foundation of Christian moral activity; they animate it and give it its special character. They inform and give life to all the moral virtues. They are infused by God into the souls of the faithful to make them capable of acting as his children and of meriting eternal life. They are the pledge of the presence and action of the Holy Spirit in the faculties of the human being. There are three theological virtues: faith, hope, and charity. (*CCC* 1812–1813)

APPLICATION: TAKING IT TO HEART

Having explored our Redemption in Jesus Christ, we can now apply this awareness to the ascetical life and see how it can help us to grow in our supernatural life with God.

The following spiritual exercises are suggested as helps in the work of the ascetical life.

Focus from the Holy Mass

Reflect upon the *Ecce, Agnus Dei:* "Behold the Lamb of God, behold him who takes away the sins of the world. Blessed are those called to the supper of the Lamb."

Consider: 1) The suffering of the long-awaited Savior; 2) The love that motivated his saving mission; 3) The kindness of the Savior in calling you to himself and inviting you to be at his banquet.

Lectio Divina *Suggestion*

Spend some time, perhaps five to fifteen minutes, repeating and breathing into your heart the following portion of the living Word of God: "When Jesus had received the wine, he said, 'It is finished.' Then he bowed his head and gave up his spirit" (Jn 19:30).

Consider: Pray upon those earth-shaking, all-powerful, awe-inspiring words, "It is finished." Reflect upon the primordial promise of a Savior. Think of the many stages of salvation history as the promise was developed and God was preparing us to receive our Savior. Let your heart be united with the Lord's. Let gratitude and hope fill your soul.

Meditation Theme

Use your spiritual imagination and compose a place. Imagine the sights, smells, sounds, taste, and touch of the environment. Allow yourself to be truly, spiritually present in that moment.

Picture the Mount of Calvary. Imagine the dirt and rocks of the hill. Feel the weather around you. Look at the color of the clothes of the people who are there. Hear the shouting and mockery. See the Lord Jesus walking up the mount. See Simon of Cyrene helping him with the Cross. Smell the blood and open wounds of his body. Let your heart shake. Imagine his frailty and brokenness. Allow yourself to see his eyes. Imagine him looking at you, only you. When the time is right, begin your colloquy, your conversation with him. Ask him the questions on your heart. Listen quietly. Love deeply. Know that the Lord is with you.

Poustinia Meditation

This method is different from other forms of prayer. The task is to clear your mind of all thoughts and attempt to think of nothing other than a simple word.

It can be repeated multiple times or simply held in our minds. Sometimes the use of a foreign word can help us stay focused. For our exercise today, focus on the word: "Redemptio" (Latin for "redemption"), or another word that has stood out to you during this chapter.

Examination of Conscience

Do I seek to love the Lord Jesus with all my heart?

Do I actively nurture my life with God through the sacraments and prayer?

Have I declared Mary my spiritual Mother and given her due homage?

Do I patiently accept suffering?

Am I prisoner to the respect of my neighbors?

Have I sought to justify or rationalize my sins?

Do I rely on the help of God's grace?

Do I meditate on the Lord's Passion and Death?

Have I sought acts of penance for my sins and those of my neighbor?

Do I quickly forgive others?

Suggested Saints and Holy Ones

As we reflect upon our redemption in Jesus Christ, it would be a noble thing to ask for the spiritual friendship and intercession of saints who were involved in the Lord's Passion and Death. In particular, we can turn to Simon of Cyrene, Veronica of the Holy Veil, and to the Good Thief. Each of these people was a consolation to our Lord during his dolorous Passion and ignominious Death.

As we seek holiness, and the internal peace that comes with it, we can turn to these holy ones and ask for their prayers and spiritual mentoring.

One of the criminals who were hanged there kept deriding him and saying, "Are you not the Messiah? Save yourself and us!" But the other rebuked him, saying, "Do you not fear God, since you are under the same sentence of condemnation? And we indeed have been condemned justly, for we are getting what we deserve for our deeds, but this man has done nothing wrong." Then he said, "Jesus, remember me when you come into your kingdom." He replied, "Truly I tell you, today you will be with me in Paradise." (Lk 23:39–43)

Three Prayers from Our Tradition

ACT OF HOPE

O my God,
relying on Thy infinite goodness and promises,
I hope to obtain pardon of my sins,
the help of Thy grace and life everlasting,
through the merits of Jesus Christ,
my Lord and Redeemer.
Amen.

PRAYER BEFORE A CRUCIFIX

Look down upon me, good and gentle Jesus,
while before Thy face I humbly kneel,
and with burning soul I pray and beseech Thee
to fix deep in my heart lively sentiments of faith, hope, and charity,
true contrition for my sins, and a firm purpose of amendment;
while I contemplate with great love and tender pity

Thy five wounds,
pondering over them within me,
having in mind the words which David Thy prophet
   said of Thee, my Jesus:
"They have pierced my hands and my feet; they have
   numbered all my bones."

LITANY OF HUMILITY

O Jesus! meek and humble of heart, Hear me.

From the desire of being esteemed,
   Deliver me, Jesus (*repeat after each petition*)
From the desire of being loved...
From the desire of being extolled...
From the desire of being honored...
From the desire of being praised...
From the desire of being preferred to others...
From the desire of being consulted...
From the desire of being approved...
From the fear of being humiliated...
From the fear of being despised...
From the fear of suffering rebukes...
From the fear of being calumniated...
From the fear of being forgotten...
From the fear of being ridiculed...
From the fear of being wronged...
From the fear of being suspected...

That others may be loved more than I,
   Jesus, grant me the grace to desire it
   (*repeat after each petition*)
That others may be esteemed more than I...
That, in the opinion of the world,
   others may increase and I may decrease...

That others may be chosen and I set aside...
That others may be praised and I unnoticed...
That others may be preferred to me in
    everything...
That others may become holier than I,
    provided that I may become as holy as I
    should...
Amen.

CHAPTER FOUR

Divine Grace

"Father, I desire that those also, whom you have given me, may be with me where I am, to see my glory, which you have given me because you loved me before the foundation of the world."

John 17:24

A DEEPER UNDERSTANDING

YEARS AGO, I WAS SPEAKING WITH a good Catholic friend about our Faith and our call to worship God in spirit and truth. After some initial conversation, my friend told me that he knew he was growing in his discipleship when worship stopped being about him. He described how the Holy Spirit broke the bubble of his own narcissism and how he began to go deeper in worship, realizing it was a call to die to ourselves and to focus all our strength and energies on God.

It was a powerful and encouraging testimony, but he wasn't done.

My friend went on to explain how he thought that he had arrived—that he now understood worship and the summons to adore and praise the living God. He then shared that he couldn't have been farther from the truth.

In summary, he told me, "After getting out of my own self-absorption, I figured things were good. Only after diving more into the mysteries of worship did I realize that I still had more growth to undergo. There was another entire horizon I didn't even know existed. I figured that I had reached a good understanding of worship because I was surrendering myself to God. I had no idea about grace. As I was opening myself up to God and trying to be a living sacrifice to him, I didn't have a clue that he was pouring his own life and power into me. I couldn't have ever imagined that such a radical, absolutely existential, body-and-soul, to-the-heart, root-and-branch regenerative transformation was happening with me as the Almighty and Ever-living God—Father, Son, and Holy Spirit—was coming to dwell within me...within me! God taking up his residence in me!"

The wording, tone, and spirit of my friend said it all. He got it. Worship is our participation in the work of Jesus Christ and the means by which we can actively share in the very life of God. It is in worship that we principally receive the gift of grace, and nothing—nothing!—can compare to this gift—the very life of God living within us! Yes, it is grace that brings about our justification and our sanctification in Jesus Christ.

Do we understand the utter importance and centrality of grace in the development of our supernatural lives? Do we realize how essential grace is for us to grow in the divine life of God?

Listen! I am standing at the door, knocking; if you hear my voice and open the door, I will come in to you and eat with you, and you with me. (Rev 3:20)

THE HOLY SPIRIT AND GRACE

The Paschal Mystery of the Lord Jesus Christ, namely, his Passion, Death, and Resurrection, has reconciled humanity to the Father and opened the life of grace to us. Grace is the unmerited favor of God. It saves us from sin, regenerates us, and makes us one of his children. Grace is the very life of God abiding within us. It is the source and nourishment of our supernatural life. It is the power of God within us that moves us to seek holiness by doing good and avoiding evil.

In the life of the Church, the reality of grace is understood within an intricate theological network of terms and explanations. Ascetical theology rightly divides grace into different types, so that we can understand what God is specifically doing within us and how we are called to respond to him. Rather than cause confusion, the theological explanation of grace is designed to give us both clarity and precision in thought and action.

What, then, is the theological explanation of grace? Where does it begin?

The teaching on grace begins with the Holy Spirit, since "no one comprehends what is truly God's except the Spirit of God" (1 Cor 2:11). It is the Holy Spirit—the Third Person of the Holy Trinity and the Love between the Father and the Son—who shows us the face of the Father (see Gal 4:6) and fulfills the saving work of our Redeemer (see 1 Cor 12:3). The Holy Spirit takes the merits of our Lord's Paschal Mystery and applies them to our hearts and to the entire body and work of the Church throughout time. He is the one who dwells within us. He is the source of all grace. The supernatural life cannot be understood or lived without his presence and help.

> The Holy Spirit is the master of the interior life. By giving birth to the "inner man," justification entails the *sanctification* of his whole being. (CCC 1995)

Admittedly, many people today might echo the early Christians of Ephesus, who said, "We have not even heard that there is a Holy Spirit" (Acts 19:2b). This is true in part because the Holy Spirit does not speak of himself, as the Lord Jesus taught us: "When the Spirit of truth comes, he will guide you into all the truth; for he will not speak on his own, but will speak whatever he hears, and he will declare to you the things that are to come" (Jn 16:13). It is also true, however, because of a widespread neglect in teaching about our supernatural lives and ascetical theology.

It is the Holy Spirit who moves in the heart of every man and woman, summoning them to fellowship with the one, true God. He calls us all to divine sonship. In his sanctifying work, the Holy Spirit moves where his divine action is needed. There is no controlling or calculating his activity among us. The Lord Jesus references this movement of the Holy Spirit when he told us: "The wind blows where it chooses, and you hear the sound of it, but you do not know where it comes from or where it goes. So it is with everyone who is born of the Spirit" (Jn 3:8). As the children of God, therefore, we can have confidence that the Holy Spirit will always be present when he's sought after, and that grace will be dispensed to us whenever its needed.

> But the Advocate, the Holy Spirit, whom the Father
> will send in my name, will teach you everything, and
> remind you of all that I have said to you. (Jn 14:26)

By understanding the presence and power of the
Holy Spirit, we can now explore the intricacies of grace.

JUSTIFICATION AND
SANCTIFYING GRACE

The first work of grace is to call us from darkness to
light. It summons us to repentance and conversion. It
shows us our spiritual death and offers us the promise
of life. When we respond to the invitation of grace, we
are offered holy Baptism. In this sacrament, our sins
are forgiven and we receive adoption from God and
become true sons of God by grace.

> Peter said to them, "Repent, and be baptized every
> one of you in the name of Jesus Christ so that your
> sins may be forgiven; and you will receive the gift
> of the Holy Spirit." (Acts 2:38)

In Baptism, we are led through the Lord's own
Paschal Mystery. By the will of the Father and the
work of the Holy Spirit, we re-live in our souls the
Lord's own Passion, Death, and Resurrection by dying
to death, accepting the crosses of the fallen world, and
being regenerated—reborn—in Jesus Christ as a new
creation (see Jn 3:1–21).

> Do you not know that all of us who have been
> baptized into Christ Jesus were baptized into his
> death? Therefore we have been buried with him
> by baptism into death, so that, just as Christ was
> raised from the dead by the glory of the Father, so
> we too might walk in newness of life. (Rom 6:3-4)

In holy Baptism, we are purified of our sins, consecrated in Jesus Christ, and restored to sanctifying grace, namely, to a familial relationship with God as our Father. As members of the human race who were separated from our Father, Baptism is our homecoming celebration (see Lk 15:20-24). In Baptism, we are adopted and restored to the house of our Father. We were dead, but now brought back to life.

> Through the power of the Holy Spirit we take part
> in Christ's Passion by dying to sin, and in his Resur-
> rection by being born to a new life; we are members
> of his Body which is the Church, branches grafted
> onto the vine which is himself. (*CCC* 1988)

In holy Baptism, as we re-live the Paschal Mystery, we are given sanctifying grace. The very grace lost by our first parents is now redeemed and given to us by the saving work of Jesus Christ. By this grace, we are made partakers of the divine nature and sharers in eternal life (Rom 8:14-17; 2 Pet 1:3-4). We were in darkness, but now dwell in God's own wonderful light (see 1 Pet 2:9).

> This knowledge of faith is possible only in the Holy Spirit: to be in touch with Christ, we must first have been touched by the Holy Spirit. He comes to meet us and kindles faith in us. By virtue of our Baptism, the first sacrament of the faith, the Holy Spirit in the Church communicates to us, intimately and personally, the life that originates in the Father and is offered to us in the Son. (CCC 683)

The restoration of sanctifying grace cannot be overestimated. This is the actual filial relationship that was lost in the Garden of Eden. This powerful grace, this relationship of son and daughter to God, is restored to us—with infinitely greater blessings—in Jesus Christ. The presence of sanctifying grace gives birth to the supernatural life in our souls. It is the beginning and the root of the life of God within us.

> The Most Holy Trinity gives the baptized sanctifying grace, the grace of *justification* ... Thus the whole organism of the Christian's supernatural life has its roots in Baptism. (CCC 1266)

Unless it is lost by mortal sin, sanctifying grace remains in our souls, which is why ascetical theology sometimes calls it *habitual grace*. Sanctifying grace introduces us to the intimacy of the Holy Trinity. It is the grace that helps us to know our worth and dignity in God, and which shows us our sonship to the Father. It is the grace by which we are made a new creation and restored to the likeness of our Father (cf. Rom 6:4; 2 Cor 5:17; Eph 4:24). For this reason, ascetical theology also calls sanctifying grace *deifying grace*, since it is the grace which makes us "like God" in Jesus Christ.

The fallen desire of our first parents at the beginning of time to be "like God" without God is now definitively corrected and the supernatural state—the likeness of God—is offered to us in total abundance by the sanctifying grace of Baptism given to us in Jesus Christ (cf. Gen 3:5; Jn 1:14-16; 2 Cor 3:18).

Having grasped the immense gift of sanctifying—deifying—grace in holy Baptism, we can now explore other aspects of grace in the supernatural life.

> Justification is the *most excellent work of God's love* made manifest in Christ Jesus and granted by the Holy Spirit. It is the opinion of St. Augustine that "the justification of the wicked is a greater work than the creation of heaven and earth," because "heaven and earth will pass away but the salvation and justification of the elect...will not pass away." He holds also that the justification of sinners surpasses the creation of the angels in justice, in that it bears witness to a greater mercy. (CCC 1994)

THE LIFE OF GRACE: SANCTIFYING GRACE

Sanctifying grace introduces us to the life of God. It transforms us into his sons and daughters and strengthens us to live according to our vocation and dignity as his adopted children. As such, by this grace, we can faithfully exercise the infused virtues of faith, hope, and love. We can respond to the promptings of the Holy Spirit, especially through his seven gifts of wisdom, understanding, right judgment, courage, knowledge, reverence, and the spirit of wonder and awe. We are also fortified to grow in goodness through the moral virtues.

Such a life, however, is not easy. We are fallen and still inclined to sin. We need the help of God. We need continual sources of grace.

In light of this fallen reality, there are other means of grace given to us: sanctifying grace in other sacraments, sacramental grace, and actual grace. Each of these has its proper function and role within our supernatural lives. Each of these graces must be sought and responded to if we are to be faithful to the ways of God.

As a start, let's return to sanctifying grace. What happens when someone commits a mortal sin and this grace is lost? Is it lost forever?

Without the merciful love of Jesus Christ, mortal sin would kill sanctifying grace within us forever. The Lord Jesus, however, has given us two sacraments of healing that come to our rescue in moments of grave sin.

The principal sacrament in such a state is Penance (commonly called Confession). This sacrament is given to us as a means of absolution and restoration. When we repent of our sins and receive the mercy of God in this sacrament, we are given sanctifying grace again. It is for this reason that ascetical theology has sometimes symbolically called Penance "the second baptism," since it effects the same return to sanctifying grace as Baptism itself originally did within our souls.

> Jesus said to them again, "Peace be with you. As the Father has sent me, so I send you." When he had said this, he breathed on them and said to them, "Receive the Holy Spirit. If you forgive the sins of any, they are forgiven them; if you retain the sins of any, they are retained." (Jn 20:21–23)

In similar fashion, for those who are sick or dying, the Anointing of the Sick also has the power to absolve sin and restore us to sanctifying grace (although this power is only given when Penance is not available).

> Are any among you sick? They should call for the elders of the church and have them pray over them, anointing them with oil in the name of the Lord. The prayer of faith will save the sick, and the Lord will raise them up; and anyone who has committed sins will be forgiven. (Jas 5:14–15)

In both cases, the Lord Jesus is ministering to us through his sacraments of healing. He is redeeming us from terminal sin and restoring us to our filial relationship with the Father. He is giving us sanctifying grace and caring for the well-being of our supernatural lives.

In addressing Baptism, Penance, and the Anointing of the Sick, however, we are led to recognize that the Lord Jesus further blessed us with four other sacraments. The four remaining sacraments are Confirmation, Holy Eucharist, Holy Matrimony, and Holy Orders.

In total, there are seven sacraments in the new and everlasting covenant given to us by the Lord Jesus. They were instituted by his Paschal Mystery so that we might know God our Father, nurture our supernatural life by his grace, and so share in his divine life into eternity. Each sacrament, therefore, participates in the Paschal Mystery. They are a seven-fold share in the Passion, Death, and Resurrection of the Lord Jesus. Each of the seven sacraments is confected by the power of the Holy Spirit for the purpose of transforming our souls and building up our supernatural lives.

As we name the sacraments, it's essential that we understand what a sacrament is. In summary, a sacrament is a visible sign of invisible grace, instituted by Christ, entrusted to the Church, and brought about by the power of the Holy Spirit.

> The sacraments are efficacious signs of grace, instituted by Christ and entrusted to the Church, by which divine life is dispensed to us. The visible rites by which the sacraments are celebrated signify and make present the graces proper to each sacrament. They bear fruit in those who receive them with the required dispositions. (CCC 1131)

While sanctifying grace is directly given by Baptism, Penance, and the Anointing of the Sick, the four other sacraments—when they are received worthily—produce an increase of sanctifying grace in our souls and deepen our supernatural lives. This is true even of the sacraments that can be repeated, such as the reception of Holy Communion (and the regular and frequent use of Confession when we are already in the state of grace).

This last point needs to be emphasized. The offering of the Eucharistic Sacrifice is the sacramental re-living of the Paschal Mystery of the Lord Jesus. It re-presents the one, historic sacrifice of the Lord Jesus to the Father by the power of the Holy Spirit within time and space.

The Eucharistic Sacrifice is the means by which the Holy Spirit extends and applies the merits of the Lord's redemption to every age and people. It is the ratification of the new and everlasting covenant of Jesus Christ. The Eucharistic Sacrifice is the source and summit of our life of sanctifying grace. We could not remain and live in sanctifying grace without the reception of Holy Communion in the Eucharistic Sacrifice. With every reception of Holy Communion, our souls deepen in sanctifying grace, in the very life of God within us.

> *Holy Communion augments our union with Christ.* The principal fruit of receiving the Eucharist in Holy Communion is an intimate union with Christ Jesus. Indeed, the Lord said: "He who eats my flesh and drinks my blood abides in me, and I in him." Life in Christ has its foundation in the Eucharistic banquet: "As the living Father sent me, and I live because of the Father, so he who eats me will live because of me." (*CCC* 1391)

The supernatural life, therefore, depends upon the worthy and frequent reception of Holy Communion, as well as the regular and frequent reception of the sacrament of Penance. The soul who seeks to love God, grow in grace, and receive eternal life, must love and regularly partake of the Lord's sacraments. If a soul does not, it will certainly fall away.

> The Church affirms that for believers the sacraments of the New Covenant are *necessary for salvation*. (CCC 1129)

It is important to note as we talk about our growth in sanctifying grace that it is not God's love that increases. The love of our Heavenly Father is already infinite and perfect. In receiving sanctifying grace, it is the capacity of our own souls to receive and live in his love that grows. Grace expands our hearts, enhances our nature, and deepens our ability to receive more of God's love and to reciprocate even more of our love to him. This is the transformative and powerful work of sanctifying grace.

THE LIFE OF GRACE: SACRAMENTAL GRACE

As we explore the depths of sanctifying grace, it might be asked: If all seven sacraments nourish sanctifying grace in our souls, why do we have seven sacraments? Couldn't there be just one sacrament?

The question indicates the primacy of sanctifying grace, while also pointing us to another type of grace, namely, to *sacramental grace*. In addition to sanctifying grace, each sacrament also carries its own unique sacramental grace.

Sacramental grace depends upon sanctifying grace, but there is a complementarity between the two. While sanctifying grace and sacramental grace possess an active dynamism between them, they are distinct graces and must be seen in their own light.

> "Sacramental grace" is the grace of the Holy Spirit, given by Christ and proper to each sacrament. The Spirit heals and transforms those who receive him by conforming them to the Son of God. The fruit of the sacramental life is that the Spirit of adoption makes the faithful partakers in the divine nature by uniting them in a living union with the only Son, the Savior. (CCC 1129)

Ascetical theology understands sacramental grace as the distinctive grace of a particular sacrament which helps us to live out and fulfill the purpose of the sacrament in the supernatural life of our souls. It is given to the baptized person who worthily receives the respective sacrament.

> And God is able to provide you with every blessing in abundance, so that by always having enough of everything, you may share abundantly in every good work. (2 Cor 9:8)

In addition, ascetical theology teaches that sacramental grace is God's promise to the recipients of the sacrament that they will receive the helps necessary to fulfill the expectations of the sacrament and so grow in the supernatural life. As such, sacramental grace is based upon the particular sacrament that's received and upon our state in life.

> But each of us was given grace according to the measure of Christ's gift. (Eph 4:7)

The understanding of sacramental grace can help us to discern and recognize the presence of God throughout the different stages and phases of life. We begin with holy Baptism, oftentimes as infants, and receive the rebirth of our souls. We receive the absolution of our sins through the sacrament of Penance when we reach the age of reason. In addition, this sacrament is a refuge to us throughout life, especially in darker and more difficult moments. We are also welcomed to participate in the Eucharistic Sacrifice and receive the Body and Blood of the Lord Jesus at the age of reason. This sacrament becomes food for the journey, a means of close union with the Lord Jesus throughout the joys and sorrows of life.

In our older childhood or younger adulthood, we petition our local bishop, as a successor of the apostles, to administer Confirmation by calling down the Holy Spirit upon us. The sacrament is given through the laying on of hands and an anointing with sacred chrism. Its graces help us to remain devoted and true to the supernatural life within us and to defend the Lord Jesus and his Church with all our strength.

In adulthood, we discern our vocation in the life of the Church. Those baptized Christians who are called to Holy Matrimony receive the grace of that sacrament to faithfully and virtuously fulfill the duties and responsibilities of the marital vocation until death separates the spouses. Those baptized Christian men who are called to Holy Orders receive the grace of that sacrament to be holy shepherds of God's people, faithfully fulfilling the commitments and obligations of the ordained state.

During times of serious illness, in old age, and when we are dying, we receive the healing and help of the

Anointing of the Sick. The graces of the sacrament remove fear and distrust and give us confidence and hope in God.

Throughout the twists and turns of the different stages of life, therefore, the sacraments and their graces are available to us. Such sacramental grace blesses us and fortifies us. It gives us the presence of God and bestows divine assistance upon us so that we can live the supernatural life throughout our pilgrim journey in this world.

> Christ instituted the sacraments of the new law. There are seven: Baptism, Confirmation (or Chrismation), the Eucharist, Penance, the Anointing of the Sick, Holy Orders and Matrimony. The seven sacraments touch all the stages and all the important moments of Christian life: they give birth and increase, healing and mission to the Christian's life of faith. There is thus a certain resemblance between the stages of natural life and the stages of the spiritual life. (CCC 1210)

In speaking of sacramental grace being given throughout our lives, it's understandable that we want to know what exactly it does in our souls.

Of the different graces that are given in the respective sacraments, the most significant manifestation of sacramental grace is the *sacramental character*. It's given in the sacraments of Baptism, Confirmation, and Holy Orders. Ascetical theology understands the sacramental character as a seal that is placed upon a person's soul which radically configures it to the Lord Jesus Christ. It is indelible, that is, a permanent and unchanging seal. It is a mark on the person's soul and a promise of God's help and assistance in living as his child through Baptism and Confirmation or selflessly serving his people through Holy Orders.

> The three sacraments of Baptism, Confirmation, and Holy Orders confer, in addition to grace, a sacramental *character* or "seal" by which the Christian shares in Christ's priesthood and is made a member of the Church according to different states and functions. This configuration to Christ and to the Church, brought about by the Spirit, is indelible; it remains forever in the Christian as a positive disposition for grace, a promise and guarantee of divine protection, and as a vocation to divine worship and to the service of the Church. Therefore these sacraments can never be repeated. (*CCC* 1121)

Other examples of sacramental grace:

▸ In the sacrament of holy Baptism, we receive sacramental graces that help us to exercise the theological virtues of faith, hope, and charity;

▸ In Confirmation, we receive the sacramental graces to remain strong in our love for the Lord Jesus, active in living the Christian way of life, and courageous in defending the gospel in society;

▸ In the Holy Eucharist, we receive the sacramental graces to grow in supernatural love of God and our neighbor;

▸ In the sacrament of Penance, we receive the sacramental grace of healing. We also receive graces to resist temptation and avoid the near occasions of sin;

▶ In the Anointing of the Sick, we receive the sacramental graces of healing. We also receive graces to fight against sickness, self-pity, and fear;

▶ In Holy Matrimony, the baptized person receives the sacramental grace to be a good and virtuous spouse and parent;

▶ In Holy Orders, the baptized male believer receives the sacramental grace to be a faithful and holy minister of the Lord Jesus and his Church.

There are other examples, many of which could be more specific. These are provided here so that we can see what sacramental grace looks like in tangible form. It's important to realize the power of sacramental grace and why it's been given to us, namely, as divine assistance for us to live and fulfill the purpose of the respective sacrament we've received.

Celebrated worthily in faith, the sacraments confer the grace that they signify. They are *efficacious* because in them Christ himself is at work: it is he who baptizes, he who acts in his sacraments in order to communicate the grace that each sacrament signifies. The Father always hears the prayer of his Son's Church which, in the epiclesis of each sacrament, expresses her faith in the power of the Spirit. As fire transforms into itself everything it touches, so the Holy Spirit transforms into the divine life whatever is subjected to his power. (CCC 1127)

Now that we have an understanding of sacramental grace, we can address and seek to grasp the reality of actual grace.

THE LIFE OF GRACE: ACTUAL GRACE

When ascetical theology defines sacramental grace, it speaks of the believer receiving "the helps" necessary to fulfill the expectations of the sacrament, and so grow in the supernatural life. These specific helps are called *actual graces.*

Admittedly, the name can be a little confusing. Aren't sanctifying grace and sacramental grace also "actual"?

In ascetical theology, the term *actual* is used in a very specialized sense. In this context, the term is used to refer to God's transient and direct action upon us ("actual") in either an internal or external way.

This explanation needs some clarification. Actual grace is a supernatural assistance from God. He bestows this gift upon us because he loves us and seeks for us to grow in the supernatural life. Unlike sanctifying grace (or sacramental grace), actual grace is not intrinsic to our souls. It is an action upon us. It is divine guidance and assistance to do some supernatural act that we cannot do without God's help. Some examples include showing kindness to someone who is unkind to us, forgiving someone who has hurt us or a loved one, and showing patience when we have been offended.

> "I am the vine, you are the branches. Those who abide in me and I in them bear much fruit, because apart from me you can do nothing." (Jn 15:5)

Actual grace does not remain with us. It comes to us in a specific moment and in a particular state of affairs. God is directing and helping us with his grace in a set time and place. Actual grace, therefore, is transient. We choose to obey or not. Once a decision is made, actual grace is either fulfilled or lost.

> Sanctifying grace makes us "pleasing to God." Charisms, special graces of the Holy Spirit, are oriented to sanctifying grace and are intended for the common good of the Church. God also acts through many actual graces, to be distinguished from habitual grace which is permanent in us. (CCC 2024)

Sanctifying grace and sacramental grace rely on the workings of actual grace. Actual grace applies the other graces to specific situations and allows our souls to grow in the supernatural life. Actual grace manifests the other graces in tangible situations and circumstances. Sanctifying grace and sacramental grace cannot be sustained without actual grace.

In a beautiful act of mercy by the Lord Jesus, actual grace still works when believers are in mortal sin. It is precisely actual grace that leads a person to repentance and conversion. When sanctifying grace is lost to mortal sin, it is actual grace that guides the person back to receiving it.

Since actual grace is manifested in the trenches of life, there are two principal ways in which it acts internally upon our intellect and will. Actual grace either illuminates our minds or inspires our wills.

In terms of an illumination of our minds, this occurs when our minds are enlightened to see what is already present, but from a divine perspective. It could also refer to a conferral of knowledge that would not otherwise be known to the person.

Some examples:

► A child is being extremely difficult and his parent questions the child's goodness, but then recalls the innocence of the child as a baby. The recollection is an actual grace that gives compassion and fortitude;

► A cancer patient is overwhelmed by treatment and feels he cannot endure the hardships anymore, but is then shown the restoration of physical health after the treatment. The insight is an actual grace that gives hope and perseverance.

> I will instruct you and teach you the way you should go; I will counsel you with my eye upon you. (Ps 32:8)

In terms of an inspiration of our wills, this occurs when our souls are assisted in making a virtuous and good decision and in persevering in the decision once it has been made.

Some examples:

► A marriage is suffering immense difficulty and the spouses are on the verge of calling it quits, but then a new wave of strength comes and they resolve to keep working to save their marriage. This is an actual grace of fidelity and perseverance.

► A drug addict wakes up from a high and feels the anguish of his body and mind. He is reminded of God's mercy and the opportunity of a new beginning. He resolves to go to Confession and to seek help in addressing his addiction. This is an actual grace of conversion and hope.

> My flesh and my heart may fail, but God is the strength of my heart and my portion forever. (Ps 73:26)

In addition to the actual graces that are given internally, there are also actual graces that are given externally as when God uses ordinary means to manifest his will and bestow his guidance to us. In this way, every person, place, or thing in creation can be a means for God to grant us this supernatural help.

Some examples:

► A husband is driving home from work and sees a sale on flowers at a local store. He decides to stop and buy some flowers for his wife. This is an actual grace giving kindness and gratitude.

► A young person is asking God for guidance in making a decision and suddenly multiple references to one of the options begin to pop up in different places. This is an actual grace giving knowledge and counsel.

> Where can I go from your spirit? Or where can I flee from your presence? If I ascend to heaven, you are there; if I make my bed in Sheol, you are there. If I take the wings of the morning and settle at the farthest limits of the sea, even there your hand shall lead me, and your right hand shall hold me fast. (Ps 139:7–10)

This is the theological understanding of actual grace. Its reality helps us to recognize the divine actions of God within our intellects and wills and within creation around us. Actual grace shows us the presence of God, his enduring love for us, and his desire for us to grow in his grace and dwell with him one day forever in heaven.

SUPERNATURAL WORLDVIEW

After walking through the truths of our original inheritance, our Fall from grace, our Redemption in Jesus Christ, and the reality of divine grace, it's important for us to appreciate the broader horizon given to us by this perspective. It is within this supernatural worldview that we can place our efforts to pray, exercise virtue, and seek holiness. Without such a perspective, we wouldn't understand what we were fighting for, or the extent of the divine assistance that's offered to us in the fight.

For the person who has labored to develop a life of prayer, perhaps even read a few popular books on "spiritual theology," or who has suffered to persevere in virtue, the frame of reference that's given to us through the truths of the supernatural life provide the necessary context for the battle for our souls. The truths of the supernatural life show us why we should fight—and keep fighting. They show us the divine helps offered to us and the purpose and rewards of the battle. What is more important, they reveal to us the divine life that is at stake in the fight, and show us the glory of having the all-holy God take up his residence and dwell within us.

The indwelling of God is the point of our lives on earth. It is the nurturing of the supernatural life in this world that aids us in being regenerated as God's children, living as members of his family, having him abide in our hearts in this life, and sharing one day in his glory forever in heaven.

The ascetical practices of prayer, study of the Sacred Scriptures, the exercise of virtue, the fostering of holy fellowship, and doing the works of mercy for the vulnerable and those in need are necessary for growth in the supernatural life, but only within the broader context of our redemption and the workings of divine grace. It is a sad reality to have a baptized Christian rally and suffer for these works of piety and mercy, but never understand their divine purpose and the supernatural transformation which they effect within us. Imagine undergoing the difficulties and sufferings of pious works without knowing the fullness of the reward that has been won for us and is offered to us in Jesus Christ!

As such, it is imperative that we understand the basics of the supernatural life. It is pressing that we grasp the action of God within us through sanctifying grace, sacramental grace, and actual grace. Such knowledge will aid us well in the battle for our supernatural life. It will give us a greater cause for tenacity and hope. It will show us the richness of God's glory and help us to persevere and to fight the good fight.

> As for me, I am already being poured out as a libation, and the time of my departure has come. I have fought the good fight, I have finished the race, I have kept the faith. From now on there is reserved for me the crown of righteousness, which the Lord, the righteous judge, will give me on that day, and not only to me but also to all who have longed for his appearing. (2 Tim 4:6–8)

"IT'S A MYSTERY!"

As we conclude our chapter on divine grace, I'm reminded of a comical conversation I had a few years ago with someone I was working with in an apostolate to those in material need. The man was taking some courses in theology and was trying to understand the different types of grace. He was confusing himself with the intricacies of their ins and outs. For some time, he kept posing exceptions, clarifying his thoughts, trying to explain the interactions of the different types of grace, posing more questions, and debating himself on particular points. Ultimately, in complete frustration, he just said to me, "I just don't understand!"

The statement caught me in a light-hearted mood, and I started laughing. I wasn't laughing at his discourse—that was actually a good example of the theological method. I was laughing at the obvious nature of his comment. When I composed myself, I said to him, "Of course, you're confused. We're all confused to some degree! Trying to understand grace is like trying to understand the very life of God. It's a mystery!"

My response brought a smile to the man's face as he recognized the point. After he shared the humor of the moment, I said to him, "If it helps, think of it like this. Sanctifying grace is being in God's family. We're his sons and daughters by grace. Sacramental grace is the specific help and expectation we have by being in God's family. Actual grace is the particular set of duties and responsibilities we have by being in the family and having set expectations of us."

The man nodded and agreed, "That's pretty good." But then he launched back into exceptions, clarifications, and self-debate. Such is life. And such is the mystery of grace, of God's supernatural life within us!

APPLICATION: TAKING IT TO HEART

Having explored Divine Grace, let us apply this awareness to the ascetical life and see how it can help us to grow in our supernatural life with God.

The following spiritual exercises are suggested as helps in the work of the ascetical life.

Focus from the Holy Mass

Reflect upon the *Orate, fratres*: "Pray brethren, that my sacrifice and yours may be acceptable to God, the almighty Father."

Consider: 1) The Paschal Sacrifice of the Lord Jesus for our redemption; 2) Our sharing in that Sacrifice through Baptism; 3) The gift of sanctifying grace in our souls and its power to transform us into the likeness of Jesus Christ.

Lectio Divina *Suggestion*

Spend some time, perhaps five to fifteen minutes, repeating and breathing into your heart the following portion of the living Word of God: "I appeal to you therefore, brothers and sisters, by the mercies of God, to present your bodies as a living sacrifice, holy and acceptable to God, which is your spiritual worship. Do not be conformed to this world, but be transformed by the renewing of your minds, so that you may discern what is the will of God—what is good and acceptable and perfect" (Rom 12:1-2).

Consider: Pray upon this summons to offer your life completely as a sacrifice to the Father in Jesus Christ. Discern what is holding you back. Name the idols that hide within your soul. Declare your life for the Lord Jesus. Surrender completely to him. Declare your life for him! Offer the sacrifice of your life.

Meditation Theme

Use your spiritual imagination and compose a place. Imagine the sights, smells, sounds, taste, and touch of the environment. Allow yourself to be truly, spiritually present in that moment.

Imagine the Upper Room. See the Lord Jesus sitting at the table with his apostles as he begins the Paschal Mystery, the font of grace for humanity. Smell the food on the table. See the tablecloths and utensils. Hear the noise from the neighborhood outside. See the apostles assembled around him. Feel the momentum of the occasion. Look at the face of our Lord as he initiates our redemption though his dolorous Passion. When the time is right, begin your colloquy, your conversation with him. Ask him the questions on your heart. Listen quietly. Love deeply. Know that the Lord is with you.

Poustinia Meditation

This method is different from other forms of prayer. The task is to clear your mind of all thoughts and attempt to think of nothing other than a simple word. It can be repeated multiple times or simply held in our minds. Sometimes the use of a foreign word can help us stay focused. For our exercise today, focus on the word: "Gratia" (Latin for "grace"), or another word that has stood out to you during this chapter.

Examination of Conscience

Do I nourish a love for the sacraments in my soul?

Do I participate in Sunday Mass and go to daily Mass whenever possible?

Am I always attentive to receiving Holy Communion in the state of grace?

Do I frequently go to Confession?

Do I encourage my loved ones to go to Confession?

Have I secured the anointing for myself or loved ones who are seriously ill or of older age?

Do I fan into flame the graces of my Baptism and Confirmation?

Do I honor those who are called to Holy Orders?

If married, am I attentive to fulfilling the vows of my sacrament?

Do I respond to the actual grace in my life?

Suggested Saints and Holy Ones

As we reflect upon the sacraments and sanctifying grace, we can turn to many saints in our tradition. In particular, we can seek the spiritual friendship and intercession of Saint Tarcisius, who died in defense of the Eucharist; Saint John of Nepomuk, who died protecting the seal of the confessional; and Saint Maximilian Kolbe, who died in service to Holy Matrimony.

As we seek holiness, and the internal peace that comes with it, we can turn to these holy ones and ask for their prayers and spiritual mentoring.

> Therefore, since we are surrounded by so great a cloud of witnesses, let us also lay aside every weight and the sin that clings so closely, and let us run with perseverance the race that is set before us, looking to Jesus the pioneer and perfecter of our faith, who for the sake of the joy that was set before him endured the cross, disregarding its shame, and has taken his seat at the right hand of the throne of God. (Heb 12:1-2)

Prayers from Our Tradition

BAPTISMAL VOWS
(for devotional renewal)

℣. Do you renounce sin, so as to live in the freedom of the children of God?

℟. I do.

℣. Do you renounce the lure of evil, so that sin may have no mastery over you?

℟. I do.

℣. Do you renounce Satan, the author and prince of sin?

℟. I do.

℣. Do you believe in God, the Father Almighty, Creator of heaven and earth?

℟. I do.

℣. Do you believe in Jesus Christ, his only Son, our Lord, who was born of the Virgin Mary, suffered death and was buried, rose again from the dead, and is seated at the right hand of the Father?

℟. I do.

℣. Do you believe in the Holy Spirit, the holy Catholic Church, the communion of saints, the forgiveness of sins, the resurrection of the body, and life everlasting?

℟. I do.

THE LAYING ON OF HANDS AND CHRISMATION AT CONFIRMATION
(for devotional reflection)

All-powerful God, Father of our Lord Jesus Christ,
    by water and the Holy Spirit
    you freed your sons and daughters from sin
    and gave them new life.
Send your Holy Spirit upon them
    to be their Helper and Guide.

Give them the spirit of wisdom and understanding,
the spirit of right judgment and courage,
    the spirit of knowledge and reverence.
Fill them with the spirit of wonder and awe in
    your presence. Through Christ our Lord. *Amen.*
N., be sealed with the Gift of the Holy Spirit. *Amen.*
Peace be with you. And with your spirit.

SAINT THOMAS AQUINAS'S
PRAYER BEFORE MASS

Almighty and ever-living God, I approach the sacrament of Your only-begotten Son Our Lord Jesus Christ, I come sick to the doctor of life, unclean to the fountain of mercy, blind to the radiance of eternal light, and poor and needy to the Lord of heaven and earth.

Lord, in your great generosity, heal my sickness, wash away my defilement, enlighten my blindness, enrich my poverty, and clothe my nakedness. May I receive the bread of angels, the King of kings and Lord of lords, with humble reverence, with the purity and faith, the repentance and love, and the determined purpose that will help to bring me to salvation. May I receive the sacrament of the Lord's Body and Blood, and its reality and power.

Kind God, may I receive the Body of Your only-begotten Son, our Lord Jesus Christ, born from the womb of the Virgin Mary, and so be received into His mystical body and numbered among His members.

Loving Father, as on my earthly pilgrimage I now receive Your beloved Son under the veil of a sacrament, may I one day see him face to face in glory, who lives and reigns with You forever. *Amen.*

ACT OF CONTRITION

O my God,
I am heartily sorry for having offended Thee,
and I detest all my sins because of thy just
    punishments,
but most of all because they offend Thee, my God,
who art all good and deserving of all my love.
I firmly resolve with the help of Thy grace
to sin no more and to avoid the near occasions of sin.
Amen.

PRAYER FOR THE
ANOINTING OF THE SICK
(for devotional reflection)

℣. Through this holy anointing may the
Lord in his love and mercy help you
with the grace of the Holy Spirit.
℟. *Amen.*
℣. May the Lord who frees you from
sin save you and raise you up.
℟. *Amen.*

VOWS OF HOLY MATRIMONY
(for devotional renewal)

I, (*Name*),
take you, (*Name*),
to be my wife/husband.
I promise to be faithful to you,
in good times and in bad,
in sickness and in health,
to love you and to honor you
    all the days of my life.

CHAPTER FIVE

The Purgative Way

Three times I appealed to the Lord about this, that it would leave me, but he said to me, "My grace is sufficient for you, for power is made perfect in weakness." So, I will boast all the more gladly of my weaknesses, so that the power of Christ may dwell in me.

2 Corinthians 12:8–9

"WHY IS IT SO DIFFICULT?"

ON ONE OCCASION, I WAS SPEAKing at a Marian conference. After my talk, I sat at my speaker's booth and spoke to people who stopped by, checked some emails, and was organizing the different materials on my table. Honestly, I was filling time and trying to be a resource to anyone who might want some guidance or spiritual counsel.

After some time passed, a woman approached the booth and asked a few initial questions. I could tell there was something else on her heart. After the small talk, she eventually opened up and said, "I'm really trying to grow in my relationship with God. I just don't understand. Why is it so difficult? I thought God would make it a little easier." As she spoke, her sincerity was clear, as was her exhaustion. I invited her to sit down, since the answer was going to take a while.

The answer included everything that is contained in the first four chapters of this book. The answer also includes what is called the purgative way. In summary, it's what I said to this woman seeking holiness: "When we start to take our supernatural lives seriously, it is only the beginning. We think we've reached some type of an end, but we're only starting the journey and the journey is a difficult one. God gives us his grace and we're called to respond to it, to fan it into a flame in our lives. We are a fallen race. Our self-love and pride are resistant to conversion. They rebel against grace and seek to sabotage its workings. We have to allow grace to purge us of our self-love and to cleanse us of our pride."

These teachings from ascetical theology were new to the woman. Maybe they are new to many in the Church today.

Our task in this chapter is to explore the purgative way, so we can understand that our decision to respond to grace and to nurture our supernatural lives will not be an easy or comfortable one. It will be difficult, but it's all worth it. By knowing the broader horizon that ascetical theology gives to us, we can see the glory and know the goodness of the battle.

> I consider that the sufferings of this present time are not worth comparing with the glory about to be revealed to us. (Rom 8:18)

FIRST CONVERSION

In ascetical theology, conversion refers to a "turning away" from sin and death and a "turning toward" grace and life. The purgative way is one of three "ways" in which we experience conversion through various stages so as to reach an ever-greater intimacy with God. The Scriptures describe this as obtaining "grace upon grace" (Jn 1:16).

The three ways of the supernatural life—the purgative, illuminative, and unitive—reflect the gradual workings of God. As with humanity and the Church in the course of salvation history, so with each of us now in the midst of the Church, God progressively reveals himself and allows his grace to transform us into his likeness.

The first conversion happens in our lives when God bestows an actual grace of some great awareness—usually through a crisis, difficulty, or a general sense of being lost. The first conversion is a gift to each of us, a type of awakening of our souls that helps us to hear the call of the Lord Jesus. It has the rich spiritual fruit of allowing us to see our complete unworthiness and our total need for Jesus Christ and the workings of grace. Although called "first," such a conversion can happen multiple times in life and can be repeated if we fall into sin or regress in our efforts to grow in the supernatural life.

> Since the initiative belongs to God in the order of grace, *no one can merit the initial grace* of forgiveness and justification, at the beginning of conversion. (CCC 2010)

If we accept the graces of a first conversion, then our soul enters the purgative way, which is the first real beginning of our cooperation with grace and a nurturing of the supernatural life within us. The purgative way is also given in later times in the spiritual life, such as after a great illumination. As such, the purgative way is an on-going means by which God leads us to abandon a life according to the flesh, walk according to his grace, and seek more faithfully to follow the Lord Jesus.

> For those who live according to the flesh set their minds on the things of the flesh, but those who live according to the Spirit set their minds on the things of the Spirit. To set the mind on the flesh is death, but to set the mind on the Spirit is life and peace. (Rom 8:5–6)

THE PHASES OF THE PURGATIVE WAY

The purgative way is an interior purification of our souls. It is a divine ordering and maturing of our self to the supernatural life given to us in Jesus Christ.

> The gifts he gave were ... to equip the saints for the work of ministry, for building up the body of Christ, until all of us come to the unity of the faith and of the knowledge of the Son of God, to maturity, to the measure of the full stature of Christ. (Eph 4:11–13)

In the purgative way, God's grace leads us through a re-living of the Paschal Mystery—Christ's own Passion, Death, and Resurrection—which purifies, heals, and reconstitutes who we are in Jesus Christ.

> I have been crucified with Christ; and it is no longer I who live, but it is Christ who lives in me. And the life I now live in the flesh I live by faith in the Son of God, who loved me and gave himself for me. (Gal 2:19b–20)

The purgative way has two principal phases within our souls: first, a time of consolation; and secondly, a time of darkness and desolation. These phases can be repeated within our souls depending on our faithfulness to grace.

As we enter the purgative way, we receive abundant actual grace of consolation. As described in ascetical theology, this phase is marked by immense comforts, joys, and encouragement. It's as if God is throwing a grand party in our souls. Such actual grace is given because the soul is just beginning to deepen in the supernatural life of God within it. God is comforting and indulging the soul to help it to persevere.

After the time of consolation, the next phase of the purgative way begins. It is much more difficult and more properly purgative. At times, a soul in this part of the purgative way might think that it is undergoing a "dark night of the soul" or a "dark night of the senses." While the person may think that such a phenomenon is happening to him, such experiences only happen at higher levels of the supernatural life (and are beyond the introductory nature of this book). For our purposes, it's worth noting that the dark night of the senses and the dark night of the soul are far more severe than the darkness that's experienced by a soul in the purgative way.

> The way of perfection passes by way of the Cross. There is no holiness without renunciation and spiritual battle. Spiritual progress entails the ascesis and mortification.... (CCC 2015)

In terms of the proper purgative process, it can be very abrupt. The consolations we once felt interiorly suddenly come to an end. The great party in our soul concludes. There is silence. Our soul feels alone. It is restless in perceived darkness. In this process, the graces of consolation are replaced by the graces of obedience (which comes from a Latin word meaning "to listen"). In this portion of the purgative way, our soul is now called to persevere through a purification of self-love and pride.

In the darkness of the purgative way, God reorients our soul and leads it to spiritual maturity. Our feelings which usually want to betray us and deceive us are spiritualized and channeled to a love of God and perseverance in the supernatural life.

> Since it belongs to the supernatural order, grace *escapes our experience* and cannot be known except by faith. We cannot therefore rely on our feelings or our works to conclude that we are justified and saved. However, according to the Lord's words—"Thus you will know them by their fruits"—reflection on

> God's blessings in our life and in the lives of the
> saints offers us a guarantee that grace is at work in
> us and spurs us on to an ever greater faith and an
> attitude of trustful poverty. (*CCC* 2005)

While our feelings may not experience it, God is
close to us in the purgative way and is able to bring
about a greater work within us than during the time
of consolation. It is very important that we realize the
place and purpose of this purgative darkness. Many
times those in this phase of the purgative way falsely
believe that it's a sign that they have done something
wrong, or have offended God, or have been abandoned
by him. None of these is true. In the purgative way,
we must exercise the infused virtues of faith, hope, and
love. We must cling to the sure knowledge of the workings of grace within us. We must persevere through this
supernatural version of surgery on our souls.

> Endure trials for the sake of discipline. God is treat-
> ing you as children; for what child is there whom a
> parent does not discipline? If you do not have that
> discipline in which all children share, then you are
> illegitimate and not his children. Now, discipline
> always seems painful rather than pleasant at the
> time, but later it yields the peaceful fruit of righ-
> teousness to those who have been trained by it.
> (Heb 12:7-8, 11)

While in the purgative way, God heals our wounds,
lessens our egotism, grows our spirit, exposes our

inordinate self-love, and names any bad spirits within us. He shows us the harm caused by sin.

In the purgative way, we struggle and wrestle to abandon sin and our wayward attraction to sin. We begin to yearn for a growth in the supernatural life. We pine to live fully as the children of God and want to love the Lord Jesus with all our being. We strongly desire to live a life in the Spirit.

> I do not understand my own actions. For I do not do what I want, but I do the very thing I hate.... For I do not do the good I want, but the evil I do not want is what I do.... Wretched man that I am! Who will rescue me from this body of death? Thanks be to God through Jesus Christ our Lord! (Rom 7:15, 19, 24–25)
>
> And those who belong to Christ Jesus have crucified the flesh with its passions and desires. (Gal 5:24)
>
> May I never boast of anything except the cross of our Lord Jesus Christ, by which the world has been crucified to me, and I to the world. (Gal 6:14)

In the purgative way, we find an interior summons to abandon a life of sin and self-centeredness and to seek a supernatural life of love and self-donation.

> Rid yourselves, therefore, of all malice, and all guile, insincerity, envy, and all slander. Like newborn infants, long for the pure, spiritual milk, so that by it you may grow into salvation—if indeed you have tasted that the Lord is good. (1 Pet 2:1–3)

The purgative way is neither easy nor comfortable. God lets us fully experience our own weakness and our total helplessness before him. There is spiritual suffering, a death to ourselves, our emotions, and our self-absorption, a total and heartfelt exercise of faith in God alone, a complete trust in him, and a radical desire to love God for himself and for no other reason. It is an outpouring of ourselves to God. It is the workings of grace forming us into an oblation, a living sacrifice, to the eternal God.

> Do not be conformed to this world, but be transformed by the renewing of your minds, so that you may discern what is the will of God—what is good and acceptable and perfect. (Rom 12:2)

As God works in our souls in the purgative way, he is present to us (although veiled) and his grace is actively working to bring forth a new identity within us. Such a process can be a time of great anxiety and restlessness. As such, the purgative way is a time for us to remain vigilant and to pray for the graces of perseverance.

> That is not the way you learned Christ! For surely you have heard about him and were taught in him, as truth is in Jesus. You were taught to put away your former way of life, your old self, corrupt and deluded by its lusts, and to be renewed in the spirit of your minds, and to clothe yourselves with the new self, created according to the likeness of God in true righteousness and holiness. (Eph 4:20–24)

After some duration in the purgative way, God will grant an actual grace of illumination. We will understand some truth of the supernatural life in a profoundly interior and robust way. It might be something we already cognitively knew or thought we understood, but the illumination deepens or brightens our understanding of it.

Ascetical theology highlights many people undergoing this illumination with mercy and hope in the initial stages of conversion. Of course, God will illuminate the soul in the areas in which it is most in need. After an illumination, it is common that the soul will be taken back to the purgative way and the process repeats itself as the soul cooperates with grace and grows in the supernatural life.

This is the journey of redemption and salvation in Jesus Christ. It is the process by which grace heals and restores the divine life within us.

> Therefore lift your drooping hands and strengthen your weak knees, and make straight paths for your feet, so that what is lame may not be put out of joint, but rather be healed. (Heb 12:12–13)

APPLICATION: TAKING IT TO HEART

Having explored the Purgative Way, we can now apply this awareness to the ascetical life and see how it can help us to grow in our supernatural life with God.

The following spiritual exercises are suggested as helps in the work of the ascetical life.

Focus from the Holy Mass

Reflect upon the response to the *Orate, fratres*: "May the Lord accept the sacrifice at your hands for the praise and glory of his name, for our good and the good of all his holy Church."

Consider: 1) The call we have to participate and to live out the sacrifice of Jesus Christ in our lives; 2) The self-sacrifice that is required to live the supernatural life in the Lord Jesus; 3) The merits we receive for ourselves and others as we live the Christian way of life and faithfully participate in the Eucharistic Sacrifice.

Lectio Divina *Suggestion*

Spend some time, perhaps five to fifteen minutes, repeating and breathing into your heart the following portion of the living Word of God: "Father, I desire that those also, whom you have given me, may be with me where I am, to see my glory, which you have given me because you loved me before the foundation of the world" (Jn 17:24).

Consider: Reflect upon this powerful prayer of the Lord Jesus in the Upper Room as he prepared for his Passion and Death. Consider the immense love he has for you and for all humanity. Think of the desire he has to share his glory with each of us. Reflect upon the purgative way. Consider its sufferings and purification. Commit yourself to walk this way with your Lord. Ask him to cleanse you of pride and self-love. Declare your unfailing love for him. Ask him to show you his glory!

Meditation Theme

Use your spiritual imagination and compose a place. Imagine the sights, smells, sounds, taste, and touch of the environment. Allow yourself to be truly, spiritually present in that moment.

Imagine the Lord Jesus in the desert being tempted by the Evil One. Feel the dryness in your throat and mouth. Hear the howling of the desert wind. Sense the sand hitting your body as the wind blows it. Feel the heat. Squint your eyes at the brightness of the sun. See Jesus alone in the desert and then being assaulted by the Evil One. Draw close to him. Be in the desert with him. When the time is right, begin your colloquy, your conversation with him. Ask him the questions on your heart. Listen quietly. Love deeply. Know that the Lord is with you.

Poustinia Meditation

This method is different from other forms of prayer. The task is to clear your mind of all thoughts and attempt to think of nothing other than a simple word. It can be repeated multiple times or simply held in our minds. Sometimes the use of a foreign word can help us stay focused. For our exercise today, focus on the word: "Labor" (*lah-bōr*, Latin for "work"), or another word that has stood out to you during this chapter.

Examination of Conscience

Am I living a self-centered life of comfort and ease?

Do I avoid the cross or suffering at all costs?

Am I willing to endure the purgative way to grow in my life of prayer?

Do I allow my faith to grow when struggling through the purgative way?

Do I persevere in the ways of God even when I don't
feel anything?

Have I accused myself of narcissism and allowed grace
to heal it within me?

Do I exercise virtue even when it brings suffering?

Have I challenged lies with the truth during times of
temptation?

Am I willing to endure any purgation if it means growing in the supernatural life in Jesus Christ?

Do I reflect upon the glory that God desires to give to
me and allow it to inspire me?

Suggested Saints and Holy Ones

As we reflect upon the purgative way, we can turn to
many saints in our tradition. In particular, we can seek
the spiritual friendship and intercession of the early
Desert Fathers and Mothers, whose wisdom is extolled
throughout the ascetical tradition. We can also seek the
help of the Doctors of Mystical Prayer, Saints Teresa
of Avila and John of the Cross. We can also petition
for the intercession of other spiritual masters, such as
Saints Thérèse of Lisieux and Therese Benedicta of the
Holy Cross (Edith Stein).

As we seek holiness, and the internal peace that
comes with it, we can turn to these holy ones and ask
for their prayers and spiritual mentoring.

> Hear, my child, your father's instruction, and do
> not reject your mother's teaching; for they are a
> fair garland for your head, and pendants for your
> neck. (Prov 1:8–9)

Prayers from Our Tradition

SUSCIPE PRAYER

Take Lord, and receive all my liberty,
my memory, my understanding,
and my entire will,
all that I have and possess.
You have given all to me.
To you, O Lord, I return it.
All is yours,
dispose of it wholly according to your will.
Give me your love and your grace,
for this is sufficient for me.
Amen.

PEACE PRAYER OF
SAINT FRANCIS OF ASSISI

Lord, make me an instrument of your peace:
where there is hatred, let me sow love;
where there is injury, pardon;
where there is doubt, faith;
where there is despair, hope;
where there is darkness, light;
where there is sadness, joy.

O divine Master, grant that I may not so much seek
to be consoled as to console,
to be understood as to understand,
to be loved as to love.
For it is in giving that we receive,
it is in pardoning that we are pardoned,
and it is in dying that we are born to eternal life.
Amen.

ANIMA CHRISTI

Soul of Christ, sanctify me.
Body of Christ, save me.
Blood of Christ, inebriate me.
Water from the side of Christ, wash me.
Passion of Christ, strengthen me.
O Good Jesus, hear me.
Within your wounds hide me.
Permit me not to be separated from you.
From the wicked foe, defend me.
At the hour of my death, call me
and bid me come to you
That with your saints I may praise you
For ever and ever.
Amen.

CONCLUSION

E'VE NOW REACHED THE END of our primer on the supernatural life. There is still an abundance of heavenly wisdom contained within the treasury of Mother Church, but the basics have been dissected and explained in this simple book.

Through its five chapters, this book has sought to provide the missing context to the many versions of spiritual theology in the Church and society today. Such a context is needed, if we are to grow in our relationship with the living God in Jesus Christ. It is a context that shows us our goodness, our fallenness, our redemption, and the powerful workings of divine grace, as well as the path of the purgative way.

The truths of the supernatural life are needed if we are to know why we should labor for a life of prayer, virtue, and holiness. If we do not understand the supernatural life, then the foundation, the goal, and the source of perseverance for a life of holiness and a relationship with the all-holy God in Jesus Christ loses its vigor, passion, and the purpose for which it has been offered to us. We need to know the whole story of our relationship with God, so that we can realize the greatness of his love and the infinite value of the supernatural relationship that he offers to us in his Son.

God's love was revealed among us in this way: God sent his only Son into the world so that we might live through him. In this is love, not that we loved God but that he loved us and sent his Son to be the atoning sacrifice for our sins. (1 Jn 4:9–10)

Whether it's acknowledged by our fallen world or not, we were made by God and for God. We are called to share in his own divine life. In spite of what our fallen minds might say to us, we do not merit such a gift, nor are we entitled to it. The supernatural life was lost but has been restored to us superabundantly in Jesus Christ. The supernatural life is received and becomes ours by the workings of divine grace. We must be willing to walk the purgative way for such grace to heal and conquer our pride and sinfulness and so share in God's life on earth and into eternity.

For by grace you have been saved through faith, and this is not your own doing; it is the gift of God. (Eph 2:8)

The task and journey of our lives is to understand what has been redeemed for us in Jesus Christ and what is generously offered to us in him.

The work of this book has been to give you the truth, to show you the beauty of truth, and to inspire in you the goodness and willingness to declare an unconditional, total "yes" to the workings of God within you. It is now your task to receive the truth, give the "yes," desire the regenerative and transformative power of grace in your life, and so fight the good fight through every sorrow and suffering, so that you can win the crown of righteousness, share in the divine nature, and dwell with God forever in eternity.

As Saint Paul taught us, we will not be like Moses, who had to veil his face whenever he left the divine presence. We have no veil. We can encounter the living God, share his supernatural life, and live in the freedom of grace, sharing glory unto glory.

> And all of us, with unveiled faces, seeing the glory of the Lord as though reflected in a mirror, are being transformed into the same image from one degree of glory to another; for this comes from the Lord, the Spirit. (2 Cor 3:18–19)

The work is before us. The stakes are high. The task is difficult. But God is with us. The power and wisdom of God is offered to us. It's time to say "yes." It's time to let grace work!

BIBLIOGRAPHY

GENERAL SOURCES

Catechism of the Catholic Church. 2ⁿᵈ edition. Washington, DC: United States Catholic Conference, 2016.

PARTICULAR SOURCES

Aumann, Jordan. *Christian Spirituality in the Western Tradition*. San Francisco: Ignatius Press, 1985.

_____. *Spiritual Theology*. New York: Continuum Press, 2006.

Bouyer, Louis. *Introduction to the Spiritual Life*. Notre Dame: Christian Classics, 2013.

Dubay, Thomas. *Igniting a Fire Within*. Cincinnati: Servant Press, 2002.

Groeschel, Benedict. *Spiritual Passages*. New York: Crossroad Publishing, 2009.

Grou, Jean Nicolas. *The Spiritual Life*. Manchester: Sophia Institute Press, 2002.

Hahn, Scott. *A Father Who Keeps his Promises*. Ann Arbor: Servant Publications, 1998.

John Paul II. *Veritatis Splendor* (6 August 1993). London: Veritas Publications, 1998.

Journet, Charles. *The Meaning of Grace*. Strongsville: Scepter Publishers, 1997.

Kirby, Jeffrey. *Lord, Teach Us to Pray: A Guide to the Spiritual Life and Christian Discipleship*. Charlotte: Saint Benedict Press, 2014.

_____. *Manual for Suffering*. Charlotte: TAN Books, 2021.

Lyddon, Eileen. *Mysticism for Beginners*. Hyde Park: New City Press, 2006.

Scheeben, Matthias. *The Glories of Divine Grace*. Charlotte: TAN Books, 2000.

Tanquerey, Adolphe. *The Spiritual Life*. Charlotte: TAN Books, 2000.

Thils, Gustave. *Christian Holiness*. Tielt: Lannoo Publishers, 1961.

Underhill, Evelyn. *Mysticism*. Stilwell: Digireads Publishing, 2005.

ABOUT THE AUTHOR

FATHER JEFFREY KIRBY, STD, is the Pastor of Our Lady of Grace Parish in Indian Land, SC. He is a moral theologian, Papal Missionary of Mercy, and an Adjunct Professor of Theology at Belmont Abbey College. Fr. Kirby is sought after as a retreat leader and conference speaker. He is the author of several books, including *Sanctify Them in Truth: How the Church's Social Doctrine Addresses the Issues of Our Time.*

Made in the USA
Las Vegas, NV
03 March 2022

44940089R00090